Thirty-Two Short Views
of
MAZO *de la* ROCHE

Mazo at Stony Lake, Ontario, summer 1948.

Thirty-Two Short Views
of
MAZO de la ROCHE

DANIEL L. BRATTON

ECW PRESS

Copyright © ECW PRESS, 1996

All rights reserved. No part of this publication may be reproduced, stored in a retrieval system, or transmitted in any form by any process — electronic, mechanical, photocopying, recording, or otherwise — without the prior written permission of the copyright owners and ECW PRESS.

CANADIAN CATALOGUING IN PUBLICATION DATA

Bratton, Daniel L., 1950–
Thirty-two short views of Mazo de la Roche

Includes bibliographical references and index.

ISBN 1-55022-274-0

1. Novelists, Canadian (English) – 20th century – Biography.*
2. de la Roche, Mazo, 1879–1961 – Biography.
I. Title.

PS8507.E43Z56 1996   C813'.52   C96-930662-8
PR9199.2.D45Z56 1996

This book has been published with the help of a grant from the Humanities and Social Sciences Federation of Canada, using funds provided by the Social Sciences and Humanities Research Council of Canada. Financial assistance has also been provided by grants from The Canada Council and the Ontario Arts Council.

Design and imaging by ECW Type & Art, Oakville, Ontario.
Printed by Imprimerie Gagné, Louiseville, Quebec.

Distributed by General Distribution Services,
30 Lesmill Road, Don Mills, Ontario M3B 2T6.
(416) 445-3333, (800) 387-0172 (Canada), FAX (416) 445-5967.

Distributed to the trade in the United States
exclusively by Login Publishers Consortium,
1436 West Randolph St., Chicago, Illinois, U.S.A. 60607.
Customer service: (800) 626-4330.

Distributed in the United Kingdom by Cardiff Academic Press,
St. Fagan's Road, Fairwater, Cardiff, Wales CF5 3AE.
(01222) 560333, FAX (01222) 554909.

Published by ECW PRESS,
2120 Queen Street East, Suite 200
Toronto, Ontario M4E 1E2.

PRINTED IN CANADA

ACKNOWLEDGEMENTS

Mazo de la Roche's previous biographers — Ronald Hambleton, George Hendrick, and Joan Givner — charted the territory that I have explored, and without their work I should not have been able to pursue my own. At the same time, the critical studies of Douglas Daymond, Dennis Duffy, Desmond Pacey, Jo-Ann Fellows, David Bell, and J.G. Snell have been of immeasurable value. Dennis Duffy has my special gratitude for having sparked my interest in Mazo de la Roche when he invited me to speak to the Zoroastrian Society of Ontario about the writer who lived in what is now the society's temple.

Inspiration came from Timothy Findley, for in responding to my questions he filled me with the wonder and respect that I have always felt in reading and teaching his novels. His words have been like mantras to me, and I have begun and ended my book with them.

Barbara Larson, in opening her door several years ago to a budding Mazo aficionado who in his ignorance thought her house might be Trail Cottage, has made Mazo and Caroline living presences. This book could not have been written without her assistance and kindness.

In Mississauga, Annemarie Hagan, Benares site-development coordinator, has been extremely helpful in providing information and making available the resources of the heritage section of the Community Services Department. Thanks also to Mr. and Mrs. Ted Gittings and David Rees for making possible my meeting with Esmée Rees. In reading over my comments about Acton, I find that I have created an impression that fails to reflect the hospitality shown me by Jessie Coles and Eric Balkind. Thanks as well to Hartley Coles, Charlotte Ironside, and Esther Taylor in Acton; and, elsewhere, to Bill and Jack Cudmore, Marjorie Tyrrell, George Luesby, Bill Smith, K. Dills, Al Moritz, Douglas Daymond, Robert Finch, Marysia Wright, Jim and Catherine Coles, Elske Albarda, and Carol Lamarre-Cummings.

I am greatly in debt to Jack Williams; Derek Hayter; Timothy Bratton; my mother, Shirley Bratton, who has supported my enthusiasms over the years; and Carol Williams-Hayter, who has proofread endless drafts. Special thanks to Mary Williams, editor for ECW PRESS.

The staff of the Thomas Fisher Rare Book Library of the University of Toronto have been extremely helpful in aiding my research, as have been the librarians at the Harry Ransome Humanities Research Center at The University of Texas at Austin. I am grateful, as well, to Senator Daniel Lang, who, as Mazo de la Roche's literary executor, has permitted me to quote from her works.

The passage heading my introduction and concluding my text is from *The Wars* by Timothy Findley (© Timothy Findley, 1977); © Pebble Productions Inc., 1986; reprinted by permission of Penguin Books Canada, Limited. The appendix is an excerpt from the book *Stephen Leacock: A Reappraisal*, edited by David Staines (© University of Ottawa Press, 1986; reprinted by permission of University of Ottawa Press). Richard Rodgers's "My Heart Stood Still" is quoted by permission of Warner/Chappell Music Canada, Limited. Passages quoted from the *Atlantic Monthly* questionnaire, as well as Mazo de la Roche's letter to Edward Weeks, are quoted by permission of the Harry Ransome Humanities Research Center, University of Texas, Austin. Ronald Hambleton's interviews with Mazo de la Roche, Caroline Clement, René de la Roche, and Esmée Rees are contained in the Mazo de la Roche Collection, Thomas Fisher Rare Book Library, University of Toronto. This extensive collection includes not only Hambleton's research materials, but also books, manuscripts, typescripts, drawings, photographs, and miscellanea donated by the estate of Mazo de la Roche. This material is quoted with permission of the Fisher Rare Book Library.

PHOTOGRAPHS: Cover photo is used by permission of Mrs. Esmée Rees; frontispiece photo, c. 1948, is used by permission of Mrs. Esmée Rees; illustration 2, 1994, is by the author; illustration 3, two drawings by Mazo Roche, is used by permission of the Thomas Fisher Rare Book Library; illustration 4, 1994, is used by permission of Carol Williams-Hayter; illustration 5, from the mid-1920s, is from Mazo de la Roche's scrapbooks, and is courtesy of the Thomas Fisher Rare Book Library; illustration 6, c. 1925, by Wilfred Coles, is used by permission of Jessie Coles; illustration 7, c. 1965, is used by permission of Mrs. Barbara Larson; illustration 8, 1994, is by the author; illustration 9, c. 1933, is courtesy of the Ontario Heritage Foundation; illustration 10 is courtesy of Mrs. Barbara Larson;

illustration 11, 1993, is by the author; illustration 12 is courtesy of the Reverend K.G.C. Rowcroft and Ronald Hambleton, and is used by permission of the Thomas Fisher Rare Book Library; illustration 13, 1934, is courtesy of Ronald Hambleton, and is used by permission of the Thomas Fisher Rare Book Library; illustration 14, from the mid-1930s, is used by permission of Mrs. Barbara Larson; illustration 15, 1936, is courtesy of Ronald Hambleton, and is used by permission of the Thomas Fisher Rare Book Library; illustration 16, c. 1962–63, is courtesy of the Sharon Temple Museum Society; illustration 17, 1958, is courtesy of Mrs. Barbara Larson; illustrations 18–19 are courtesy of the Thomas Fisher Rare Book Library; and illustration 20, 1994, is by the author.

TABLE OF CONTENTS

Acknowledgements 5
List of Illustrations 11
Introduction 13

Thirty-Two Short Views of Mazo de la Roche 21

Appendix 168
Notes 171
Chronology 172
Works Cited 177
Index 181

LIST OF ILLUSTRATIONS

	Mazo de la Roche	cover
1.	Mazo at Stony Lake, Ontario, summer 1948	frontispiece
2.	The Mazo de la Roche historical marker at Fairy Lake, Newmarket	22
3.	Two drawings by "Mazo Roche"	31
4.	Originally a millpond powering a flour mill, Acton's Fairy Lake was given its name by Sarah Secord. Mazo transformed it into the lagoon in *Delight*	64
5.	Mazo in communion with Trail Cottage in the 1920s	70
6.	An old photograph of Beverley, the Beardmore house in Acton, now demolished	74
7.	Benares in the 1960s: "The old red house, behind the shelter of spruce and balsam, drew into itself as the winter settled in" (*Jalna*)	76
8.	Captain Skynner's The Anchorage, an 1830s Regency cottage in Clarkson	83
9.	René and Esmée, possibly at Benares, in the early 1930s. From the Harris scrapbooks	84
10.	An 1814 portrait of Major General John Harris (1760–1833), by Charles Allingham. Allingham exhibited at the Royal Academy and Dublin Gallery. The major was the father of James Beveridge Harris, Benares's patriarch	88
11.	St. Peter's Anglican Church (built in 1887) today. The church's first rector was Reverend James Magrath, whose granddaughter Mary married Arthur Harris, son of James Beveridge Harris ..	91
12.	The Rectory, Hawkchurch, which was the setting of *Beside a Norman Tower*	109
13.	Mazo and Caroline Clement revisiting Rochedale in 1934. The photograph is inscribed to Dora and Hugh Eayrs, "with our love"	110

14. René and Esmée in southwestern England in the 1930s 114
15. Playbill announcing the opening of *Whiteoaks* at London's Little Theatre of the Adelphi, 13 April 1936 120
16. The Sharon Temple. Mazo's great-grandfather, after unveiling the golden ball, "sang, in a voice like an angel's, a hymn of dedication" (*Ringing the Changes*) 125
17. The photograph Mazo sent the Harrises with her Christmas card in 1958. The golden retriever, named Tawny, belonged to René 144
18. Edward Weeks's letter of 7 September 1956 rejecting Mazo's plan to have a photograph of her hands in *Ringing the Changes* 151
19. Letter dated 12 September 1956 in which Lovat Dickson, Mazo's editor at Macmillan, concurs with Weeks (see fig. 18) 152
20. The Mazo de la Roche memorial window, St. George's Church, Sibbald Point 165

INTRODUCTION

> You begin at the archives with photographs. . . . The boxes smell of yellow dust. You hold your breath. As the past moves under your fingertips, part of it crumbles. Other parts, you know you'll never find. This is what you have.
> — Timothy Findley, *The Wars*

There are parts of any person "you know you'll never find." The conclusion reached by the narrator of Timothy Findley's novel, though embedded in a fiction, applies to any life. This biography acknowledges from the beginning the impossibility of completely knowing its subject. I have therefore sought a form that can appropriately contain the various fragments that I have pieced together from one person's life. In frankly acknowledging — indeed, exploiting — the limitations inherent in my undertaking, I hope that I have allowed something of the real Mazo de la Roche to emerge.

I have accordingly borrowed a term from Northrop Frye, who borrowed it from Claude Lévi-Strauss, to characterize my approach: *bricolage*. Frye defines it in *The Great Code* as "a putting together of bits and pieces out of whatever comes to hand." In my book, I have drawn extensively upon Joan Givner's feminist/psychoanalytical biography of de la Roche published in 1989, as well as Ronald Hambleton's and George Hendrick's earlier portraits. To the insights of these writers I have added my own sometimes idiosyncratic observations.

To return to the matter of real versus imaginary subjects, I found, in delving into the life of Mazo de la Roche, that the line between fiction and nonfiction quickly blurred. Mazo's life was one of her most imaginative stories. We all, of course, devise our own narratives, but Mazo was in a league of her own, up there with Jay Gatsby. The discrepancies between the fact and fiction of her life were borne home when I asked an English friend who frequents Devon, where de la Roche lived from 1929 to 1935, to find out what he could about her residency there. I received, courtesy of the Exeter Central Library, the usual biographical data from an early edition of *Twentieth Century Authors*; but in reading it I again realized how successful Mazo was in promulgating her Platonic conception of herself. It is worth examining the entry in detail.

It begins "de la Roche, Mazo," yet its subject was simply born Mazo (known as Maisie) Roche. This is followed by the year of birth; it is listed as 1885, and is not only at odds with the date on her gravestone — 1888 — but it also, more importantly, conflicts with that on record — 1879. Mazo's place of birth is then given as Toronto. Again incorrect: contrary to nearly every account of her life, Mazo Roche was born in Newmarket, then a village north of Toronto.

The next part of the entry bears quotation in full, for after naming William Richmond and Alberta (Lundy) de la Roche as Mazo's parents — neither *ever* used the de la Roche patronymic — it states that the author "spent her childhood on her father's fruit farm in Ontario. She hated the city and loved the country, where, a sensitive, shy, and often lonely child, she grew up among horses, dogs, and other pets. . . . [She] was utterly unfitted for city life when her father died and they had to leave the farm and go to Toronto to live." While it is true that Mazo's family lived for five years on a fruit farm near Bronte, Ontario, they did not do so until Mazo was in her thirties; and if she was "utterly unfitted" for city life, it is curious that she lived in Toronto for the better part of her youth, and insisted that the city was her birthplace.

The entry then incorrectly gives 1918 as the date of Alberta Roche's death, which occurred in 1920, and claims that as a result of her demise Mazo and her cousin (Caroline Clement, her intimate companion) had to give up "their beloved cottage," when in fact they did not even inhabit Trail Cottage in Clarkson until 1924, selling it in 1946. The remainder of the biographical entry, dealing with the successful years after de la Roche's *Jalna* won the ten-thousand-dollar *Atlantic Monthly* prize in 1927, is more accurate. Why alter a success story?

One might argue that this particular source may simply be inaccurate, but an indication of how directly Mazo and Caroline were involved in such distortions is Miss Clement's responses to a questionnaire her cousin received from her publisher in 1927, now part of the Edward Weeks Papers at the University of Texas (an appropriate repository, given the regional provenance of the tall tale). Caroline gives Toronto as Mazo's place of birth and maintains that the year of her birth is "uncertain"; claims that a notable ancestor was guillotined during the French Revolution (as Givner points out, Uncle Frank Lundy's head *was* nearly severed when he was killed in a gruesome industrial accident in Newmarket!); says that her cousin was privately educated, "with an erratic dash or two into the University of Toronto," when, in fact, after some desultory study in small private day schools, Mazo attended public school and then Parkdale Collegiate in Toronto prior to her erratic dashes into university; and includes, under the heading of "Tastes," "mingling with good-natured city crowds," an odd pastime for one "utterly unfitted" for urban life, though the remark *is* followed by the phrase "hobnobing [sic] with simple country folk."

While many of Caroline's responses were clearly written tongue in cheek, more amusing is Mazo's assertion in her autobiography, *Ringing the Changes*, that "Caroline filled in the form as best she could, with only a few mistakes." It is this penchant for exaggeration and out and out lying that makes de la Roche (and Caroline, for that matter) such a fascinating, if ultimately enigmatic, object of study.

One of my favourite examples of this deliberate dissemination of untruths is the profile of the author of *The Thunder of New Wings* that appeared in *Chatelaine* in June of 1933, when Mazo's unsuccessful second novel, refused by her publishers, began serialization. According to *Chatelaine*'s blurb, which was clearly written in consultation with the author, Mazo's parents died when she was "still a young girl," leaving her, an only child, alone in the world. Mazo was already into her forties when her mother died in 1920: compared to this distortion, her usual inaccuracies regarding her place of birth and French Royalist family background pale. What, one may ask, caused Mazo to introduce such bizarre fabrications into her life story?

Certainly Mazo and Caroline's well-guarded world — and how the two cousins cultivated this air of secrecy, with Mazo listing privacy as her hobby! — reveals more than a dislike of publicity, more than a contempt for the crudities of self-promotion. The mystery that the two women embroidered protected their unconventional relationship; it hid from view certain aspects of their family's less than glamorous past. It created, instead, an aura of romance; it exacted revenge for years of hardship, illness, and sexual-social marginality. Most of all, Mazo's imagination allowed this devoted pair to make the stories that many of us share as children, and then leave behind, the reality of their adult life.

The photographs, the interviews, the newspaper articles stored with the Mazo de la Roche Collection at the University of Toronto tell one a good deal. They also withhold so much. On one hand, the archives reveal an intimidating presence; old tapes of Ronald Hambleton interviewing Mazo eerily bring forth a chilling, rather cruel voice from the Edwardian past. On the other hand, the same voice quickly betrays vulnerability, an almost pathetic awareness that time has passed this person by. The same is true of the recollections stored away in what seems an endless number of folders. Some people remember Mazo as terrified of life, incredibly nervous, unable to cope with everyday realities. Others recall her strength, her occasionally vicious tongue, her wit, her laughter, her style.

After Mazo's death, Caroline Clement (who outlived Mazo by over ten years) attempted to dissuade Hambleton from pursuing his biography. She wrote to him in 1965, saying that Mazo's "was a most interesting and unusual personality — changeful but never uninteresting. Such a personality cannot be presented from hearsay."[1] Now hearsay is what we are left with. In speaking to people who hold clues to the past — Esmée Rees, Mazo's adopted daughter; Barbara Sayers Larson, her old neighbour in Clarkson; Robert Finch, whose name inspired her favourite character — I have pieced together a life, always aware of the pieces left out. Miss Clement objected to anyone writing of her cousin who did not have personal knowledge of her, but whenever possible I have tried to let Mazo speak for herself, because who she was, I believe, is best expressed through her own writing.

A final word: Caroline and Mazo vehemently objected to the use of Miss de la Roche's first name in discussions of her work. Although I do not feel bound by their prejudices and predilections in this and other matters, I wish to convey no disrespect in speaking of "Mazo." We've belittled her talent, we've ridiculed what have been seen as her affectations, and now, in English Canada, we've all but forgotten her. Yet, as Timothy Findley has observed, Mazo was an icon. She was, quite simply, Mazo.

Though at times her writing enrages me, with its hidebound colonialism and arrogant dismissal of egalitarian ideals, I inevitably find myself surrendering to the power of her characters, to the magic she evokes in creating a place. I will always be haunted by Jalna, for Mazo's old house is more real to me than the highways and shopping malls that have torn the heart out of the landscape she loved.

Thirty-Two Short Views
of
MAZO *de la* ROCHE

Beginnings

In *Ringing the Changes*, published in 1957, Mazo de la Roche argued that the more that is written about a person, the less that person will be understood: "It seems to me that even two biographers can make an enigma — a mystery of any man, no matter how open his life." Mazo's life has already been explored by three biographers, and it was, as I have already indicated, anything but open, being surrounded by conflicting dates and testimony.

Still, to echo Findley, "This is what you have." Mazo de la Roche (Mazo Louise Roche) was born in her grandfather's house in Newmarket, Ontario, on 15 January 1879. By Mazo's account, she should not have arrived in the world at her Grandfather Lundy's, but at home; however, scarlet fever had confined her mother to bed under the parental roof.

Alberta Lundy Roche's only child weighed a mere three and one-half pounds. A blizzard raged outdoors, the temperature plummeting to minus twenty degrees Fahrenheit. There is a historical marker commemorating Mazo de la Roche's birth in Newmarket (fig. 2). It stands on the northern shore of Fairy Lake at the foot of Prospect Street, on which Daniel Lundy's old house was located. Imagine the snow gathering in the branches of the trees and drifting onto the lake at dusk. Enshrouded by the deepening twilight, Newmarket lies undisturbed by the horseless carriage. The howling wind is the only sound as Great-Aunt Fanny's husband, Dr. Bradford Patterson, who appears as Dr. Morgan Clemency in *Growth of a Man*, carefully descends the Lundys' front steps. Guided by his gold-headed cane and bundled in a sealskin topcoat, he makes his way through the heavy snow. *Nature speaks a silent language in the writing of Mazo de la Roche: to enter her world we need to listen to these unformed words.*

FIGURE 2

The Mazo de la Roche historical marker
at Fairy Lake, Newmarket.

To return to the photograph. Were we to look down, we would see the lake, a major force in Mazo's writing, symbolizing unrestrained life and the unfathomable otherness of the natural world. Looking up, we see the oak, its breadth and its gnarled branches suggesting the attributes Mazo most admired in humans — rugged individuality and dogged endurance, the very essence of the Whiteoaks of Jalna. On the spine of the dust jacket of her autobiography, an oak leaf is printed beneath the author's name: it is not merely decorative.

There is also significance in the circumstances surrounding Mazo's birth. That she was not born in her parents' home is certainly prophetic. Her mother, she tells us in *Ringing the Changes*, moved seventeen times during her marriage, and Mazo's life after her parents' deaths was equally frenetic, marked by one move after another, a restless quest for home. By the end of her eighty-two years, her Ontario addresses had included Newmarket, Aurora, Richmond Hill, Galt, Acton, Bronte, Clarkson, Oakville, York Mills, Forest Hill, and Toronto, where she lived in Yorkville, Parkdale, High Park, and what is now the urban core. She summered at Lake Simcoe and Georgian Bay, as well as in Quebec, Nova Scotia, and New England; she also spent a winter and spring in Boston's Beacon Hill. In the 1930s, when she called England home, Mazo stayed at nineteen different residences. Her travels were extensive. She journeyed to the United States and western Canada and made (again!) nineteen sea voyages to numerous ports, from the Caribbean to North Africa to Europe, with extended stays in Naples and Taormina, Sicily.

In a different vein, also worth noting in relation to her birth are Mazo's comments about her father. It was William Richmond Roche who named her — after "a girl to whom he once had been attached." And, a little later, he told his wife he'd be happy to help with "almost anything" except "push[ing] the pram" (*Ringing*). His seemingly innocuous banter reminds us that from the beginning of her life Mazo's father demonstrated a strongly demarcated sense of the masculine and feminine, one that informed Mazo's writing, both fictional and nonfictional, and that most certainly contributed to the shaping of her sexual identity.

Yet another aspect of her early background that the author of

Ringing the Changes emphasizes is the importance of ancestry, race, and blood. Ronald Hambleton's biography offers a very detailed tracing of Mazo's genealogy; indeed, its thorough treatment caused Caroline Clement to complain to Hambleton after the book's completion in 1966 that the reader has "to push his way through too much family," thus leaving him or her with no inkling of what sort of people Mazo's relations really were. In her letter to Hambleton (written in 1966), Miss Clement addressed this deficiency by asserting that Mazo's father's family — on his mother's side, the Bryans — "had little money and less business ability," but "were tall, good-looking (the dark Irish type)[,] light-hearted and pleasure-loving." She added that they had "deep, musical voices and dearly loved to talk." Not surprisingly, it was the blood of this side of the family that Mazo believed flowed in her veins. These essential traits, Caroline felt, were what the reader needed to know; as for the Lundys and Willsons, the Newmarket-area clans that spawned Mazo's mother, Caroline believed they had passed on little to her cousin: "The Lundys were fine people, but [Mazo] was quite unlike them though devoted to her Lundy grandparents."

Our concern is with the role Mazo's family played in her writing, for not only did her relations strongly affect her vision as an artist, but they also provided inspiration for her characters. For example, H. (Rache) Lovat Dickson, Mazo's close friend and editor at Macmillan for twenty years, asserted in an interview with Hambleton (now held in the Mazo de la Roche Collection, along with a number of other Hambleton interview tapes) that the Whiteoaks were based upon de la Roche originals, concluding, "I think they are idealized conceptions of ancestors whom she only just knew but had heard about, but if she hadn't had the sort of family background that she had, then she couldn't have written the sort of books that the Whiteoaks books are." Dickson went so far as to suggest that all the main characters in the Jalna novels were based on Mazo's ancestors.

Although both Caroline and Mazo discounted the influence of Alberta Lundy's blood relations upon the formation of Mazo's personality and the development of her characters, the branches of this side of the family tree deserve our attention. Interestingly, Mazo acknowledges in her autobiography that her mother's people were closer to her than her father's. It was to the Lundys' ancestral soil, Devon, that she turned when she felt the need for a spiritual homeland, both in her writing and her travels. This leads us to the common ground between the Lundys and the Willsons, the branch of the family that connected the two cousins.

What the Lundys and Willsons shared was United Empire Loyalist ancestry. The family of Sylvester Lundy, which had emigrated to New England from Devon in the seventeenth century, fled to Nova Scotia at the outbreak of the American Revolutionary War. There Mazo's great-grandfather, a staunch Loyalist, had married into another Loyalist family. Hiram Willson, Mazo's grandmother's father, had also wed a Loyalist, one whose forbears were Philadelphians. Mazo claimed that on the maternal side of her clan there were six generations of United Empire Loyalists. Of her four great-grandparents, three were of Loyalist descent; the fourth, her great-grandfather Willson, of English parentage and a military background, sired a son who married into yet another Loyalist family, the Clements.

For all of Caroline and Mazo's talk about the latter's affinity with her father's family, her mother's forbears may very well have been the most important influence upon her writing. While the Whiteoaks are singularly free of Loyalist associations — Jalna's founders arriving from the Old World — they represent the very traditions worshipped by Mazo's maternal ancestors. Jalna embodies the Loyalist myth. It is the stuff of every uprooted, displaced Loyalist's dreams.[2]

Notice the word "myth": the Loyalist "tradition" and the Loyalist "myth" are often used interchangeably. Both refer to an earlier, glorious age, and thereby involve us in yet another myth — the pastoral, defined by Northrop Frye in *The Bush Garden* as "the vision of a social ideal," which "in its most common form is associated with childhood, or with some earlier social condition . . . that can be identified with childhood." When the Loyalists were expelled from the United States and thus robbed of their identity, they were forced to invent one, placing great emphasis on family ties (obvious symbolism here — no breaking with the father); hierarchical authority and inherited power; and passionate devotion to the land (see Fellows).

The emotional experience of Mazo's maternal forbears included a profound sense of loss (the Lundys never recovered the prosperity and wealth they reputedly enjoyed in New England), and Mazo learned from an early age to venerate England as the symbolic fountainhead. The first chapter of *Ringing the Changes*, which so firmly establishes the Loyalist background of Mazo's family, goes a long way towards illuminating her innate conservatism. Mazo's Tory sympathies were, however, balanced by another aspect of loyalism: an emphasis on instinct and the irrational. This helps to explain the tribal nature of the Whiteoaks. Renny is family chieftain, his position enforced not only by his inherited authority but also by an elemental power recognized by those within and without the walls of Jalna.

Then there is Mazo's first book, a collection of short stories titled *Explorers of the Dawn* and set in an English cathedral town — even though Mazo had not, at that time, even set foot on English soil. Its pastoralism is indicated by its subject matter — lost childhood — as well as its setting — an austere town constructed of stone in which three boys find themselves all but incarcerated, separated from their very English father and their old country home "with its stretch of green lawn, the dogs, the stable with the sharp sweet smell of hay, and the pigeons, sliding and 'rooketty-cooing' on the roof."

After *Jalna* met with great initial success, Mazo left Canada to spend the 1930s in England. While the outbreak of World War II was the ostensible reason for her return, one might infer that she made the same discovery there that those eighteenth-century Loyalists who sailed to England rather than coming to Canada had made before her. As long as the Loyalist remains on this side of the Atlantic (where streets are frequently named after British statesmen and royalty, and towns after British hamlets and cities), the identification of the colony with the mother country remains unchallenged. On the other side of the pond, however, the realization that Canadians do not strike the English as being much different from Americans sets in, revealing the myth for what it is. This is not to say that Mazo and Caroline did not enjoy England — they *adored* England, and were never happier than when they finally bought a house in Windsor, where they could be close to the royal family. But observers they remained, never really becoming part of the social fabric.

Deny it though she might, Newmarket was Mazo's home, and it is interesting that towards the end of her time in England she wrote her Newmarket novel, *Growth of a Man*. Based on the life of forest and fisheries magnate H.R. MacMillan, who was related to Mazo through the Willsons, this novel is proof that her maternal forefathers did indeed work their way into her narratives. Although we might expect the life of the family of young Shaw Manifold, MacMillan's fictional counterpart, to reflect the domestic life of Mazo's distant cousin, Shaw's grandfather bears a marked resemblance to Mazo's grandfather Daniel Lundy. There is one passage in *Growth of a Man* in which Shaw's grandfather, Roger Gower, directly suggests Grandfather Lundy, for on his fiftieth wedding anniversary the blue-eyed, richly bearded Gower throws his arms around his brother, Merton, and dances about the dining room with him, astonishing the gathered family with his animation and dexterity. Mazo's blue-eyed, fully-whiskered grandfather, in the opening pages of *Ringing the Changes*, embraces *his* brother, Dr. John Lundy, and capers about the room in the same fashion.

Still, the Lundys were, by all accounts, fairly ordinary people, causing Mazo to revel in the mystery of her father's family which, though she was not as close to its members, was infinitely more appealing in terms of its dramatic value. For example, she refers time and again to the scholarly attributes of her grandfather, John Richmond Roche, who supposedly surrendered his Gallic surname to placate her grandmother's Loyalist relations. That he abandoned Mazo's grandmother and her sons twice and left after his death a box full of love letters documenting his amours south of the border does not seem to have diminished Mazo's fascination with her grandsire one iota. To her, he embodied culture. John Richmond Roche's obituary stated that he had been a professor of mathematics at Newton University in Baltimore. Hambleton went to great lengths to prove that no such university existed, and that John Richmond Roche was not a faculty member at the newly founded Johns Hopkins University or the University of Maryland, yet the facts hardly seem to matter — it is what Grandpa de la Roche stood for that counted for Mazo. Like her father's younger brother François — nicknamed the Marquis because of his affected Gallicisms — she must have found her grandfather's boxes of leather-bound books in dead languages a symbol of everything that Newmarket was not.

The most powerful presences in Mazo's reminiscences of her paternal forbears, however, are the women — as tall and good-looking as their men, and a good deal more formidable. Sarah Danford Bryan, Mazo's great-grandmother, ruled not only her children but also her children's children, including Mazo's father. She was clearly the prototype of Adeline Whiteoak, as suggested by correspondences between their portraits — Mazo's great-grandmother's, brought to Canada from Ireland, and Adeline's, transported from London to Jalna. Yet Mazo's descriptions of her grandmother also suggest Gran Whiteoak; Sarah Bryan Roche's way of carrying herself like a rudderless but impressive ship at eighty-seven reminds us of Adeline Whiteoak's setting forth in *Jalna* "like some unseaworthy but gallant old ship" in her ninety-ninth year.

"These were in every way a contrast to my mother's people . . ." Mazo begins her chapter on her father's family. Whereas Alberta Lundy's origins were boringly Anglo-Saxon, W.R. Roche's were exotically French and Irish, "the tall dark Spanish type of Irish." His people were impulsive, demonstrative, and passionately in love with life itself. Yet Mazo describes her parents as having possessed much in common:

> Both loved country life, horses and dogs — she in moderation — he to excess. Both were extravagant in dress — for her, the most expensive shops — for him, the best tailor. Both — with the best intentions — ran up bills which afterward they found difficult to pay. Both were extravagantly generous to friends and family. Both demonstrative in affection. She quick in anger and retort. He slow to anger, forbearing, but when roused, violent in his rage. Both forgiving and ready to be won by kindness.

When she writes of the influence of her parents' natures, however, Mazo — quite unconsciously, it would seem — presents her father's legacy as glowingly positive, her mother's as burdensomely negative.

From her mother, she implies, she received her oversensitivity, her vibrating nerves, her ill health. After contracting scarlet fever in 1879, Alberta Roche never completely regained her resistance; after her nervous collapse in 1903, Mazo never completely regained her strength. Moving to Galt in search of physical and psychological well being, Alberta steadily declined; confined to bed as treatment for the "blight" that had descended upon her, Mazo moaned to her uncle that she was "done for," that she'd "never be well again." The reader of her autobiography begins to perceive an equation (femininity equals . . .) that would have sent Virginia Woolf right up the wall.

From her father, on the other hand, Mazo sees herself as having received her penchant for adventure, her Gallic excesses, her intense love of animals and nature. Reflecting on her mother's long years of illness, Mazo marvels at how her father never complained, remembering how one day, when she entered her mother's room after an invigorating game of tennis, she found her father quietly imparting to his wife "the strength of his presence." She then wonders "How often his stalwart frame must have hungered for something beyond the sick-room!"

Yet, however powerful and irrepressible the influence of Mazo's father and mother upon her development as a woman and as a writer, the most important event of her life occurred on the frosty January afternoon a Lundy uncle arrived at the family home and, unravelling layers of shawls as though he were performing a conjuring trick, revealed to those assembled Mazo's younger cousin. *[Enter Caroline Clement. Let the Play begin.]*

The Play

The scene of Caroline's arrival, which serves as the prologue to *Ringing the Changes*, is best read as fiction. Mazo claims to have been seven years old that January afternoon, yet if we accept as accurate Caroline Louise Clement's gravestone, on which is engraved the birth year 1888, we must conclude that Caroline had not even been born when Mazo was seven. But then Caroline may have subtracted nine years from her age, as well, according to *Genealogies of the Builders of the Sharon Temple*, which lists her birthdate as 4 April

1879. However, Esmée Rees, Mazo's adopted daughter, believes Caroline to have been about ten years younger than her cousin, and this corroborates Joan Givner's contention that Mazo was probably sixteen years old at the time of the scene described in her autobiography. The exact date of Caroline's appearance in the Lundy household will likely remain a mystery.

Ringing the Changes is notorious for its failure to provide the reader with actual dates — once Mazo had determined to subtract nine years from her life, she had opened a can of worms. The obvious solution was to avoid providing dates before 1927, the year she won the *Atlantic Monthly* prize; as a result of that award, she came under public scrutiny. Yet she continued to shroud her life in obscurity.

Since Mazo was about to describe activities of the two cousins more appropriate to childhood, she may have chosen to present herself as preadolescent; it's probably wise to maintain a healthy scepticism about the rest of the autobiography's prologue, as well, though its details hardly matter if we accept it as more of a Victorian set piece than a slice of real life. For within Uncle George Lundy's bundle — and it must have been a fairly hefty one to carry about — reposes a fairy-tale princess, her silvery hair hanging "like limp petals of a flower." Uncle George's dramatic unveiling of a blue-eyed, angelic little waif is, as George Hendrick has suggested, almost a parody of Mr. Earnshaw's presentation of Heathcliff at Wuthering Heights.

Mazo actually mentions the Brontës in her autobiography, linking the creators of the imaginary places Angria and Gondal to the scene of the prologue. No sooner is Caroline unwrapped than she and her cousin race upstairs to forge an immediate and "delicious intimacy," far away from the adult world below. As the January sunset reddens the chilly walls, the hitherto lonely girl shares with her new companion her deepest secret, the Brontësque fantasy world of the Play.

This Play — or Game, as Mazo sometimes called it — is at the very centre of *Ringing the Changes*; the author was, in fact, deaf to any changes Edward Weeks, her editor, suggested regarding her references to it. Its influence upon her imagination, she infers, was inextricably connected to her writing. Indeed, until the end of Mazo's days, the world within was her "vivid reality" — the world

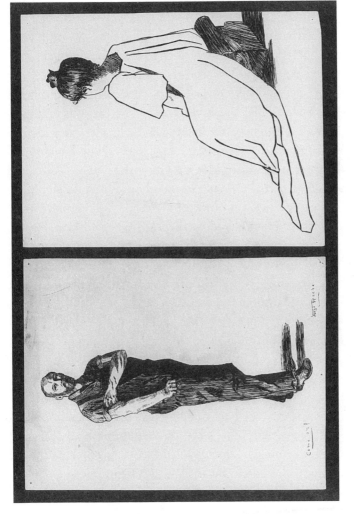

FIGURE 3

Two drawings by "Mazo Roche."

without "unreal." And Caroline's contribution to this inner kingdom was immeasurable.

It was as though Mazo had been waiting all along for her cousin's arrival. Earlier, she had had a dream — an "extraordinarily vivid dream" — from which she had awakened with the feeling that a part of herself remained submerged. And something else had been excavated in this journey into the unconscious, as well, knowledge that had made her different. The plot line of the dream was indistinct, but she remembered the characters — significantly, six males, two of whom were boys. Until Caroline appeared as the receptive "crystal goblet" beneath her cousin's "tap," however, Mazo did not guess the depth of the Play's reservoirs. Now the cast was enlarged, under Caroline's influence, to include a little girl, and then a woman. An "orgy of new characters" followed. These female roles were clearly created for Caroline; we know that when Mazo and Caroline put on an actual play at a friend's house in Parkdale, Mazo played a dashing cavalier, Caroline an innkeeper's daughter.

Figure 3 consists of two surviving drawings by Mazo Roche. Notice the artist's representation of the sexes: the male is standing, assertively posed, his sleeves rolled up for action; the female is seated with her back demurely turned to us. The Roche signature to the right beneath the burly man indicates the early date of the drawings, and the man himself suggests a character from the Play. We will return to the words in the lower left corner in a moment, for they link the male figure to an important scene in *Ringing the Changes*.

From the beginning, Mazo and Caroline established a secret life, carefully hidden from the adult world. Twice in the autobiography their intimacy is threatened by members of the family, and both times Mazo expresses their sense of being caught in the act. The first invasion happens in the prologue, while Mazo is discovering the joy of having a youthful companion. As she and Caroline touch heads while reading — appropriately — *Through the Looking-Glass* in the sunlit room, they hear Aunt Eva's unwanted step on the stairs (even the fox terrier jumps off the bed). Mazo confides to the reader, "At once she made us feel we had been caught in doing something naughty"; after the stern Aunt Eva has interrogated Caroline and departed, the two girls laugh until they cry.

The second of these intrusions occurs when Mazo and Caroline hide themselves in the darkness of the parlour and become "entranced" by the Play. Mazo suddenly senses her Aunt Eva and her father behind the curtain in the doorway; her "acute ears" hear her aunt say to her father, "Come on — let's find out what they're up to." Quickly springing to her feet, "as frightened as though I had been caught in something wicked — fearful that our Play might be stopped," Mazo, who has been playing the part of a powerful man becomes, "in a flash, a frightened child." Fortunately, her beloved father — always to the rescue — effectively tells Aunt Eva to mind her own business, and the girls resume their Play.

The details of this particular part of the Play warrant our attention. When Mazo perceives the presence of the adults, she is following a stage direction that Blount, one of her favourite characters, should grip the arms of a chair so hard that his knuckles turn white. In response to Aunt Eva's voice, Mazo passes from gripping the arms of her chair, in "manly resolution," to feeling the "sweat of humiliation" on her maidenly brow; but Caroline, always less prone to perturbation, commands, once the coast is clear, "Come on . . . be Blount again." And so, Mazo writes, "in the darkness we turned once more to the rapture of our Play." Is the man in figure 3 Blount himself, his hand clenched, responding to Caroline's command?

The Play thus allowed the cousins to live a "fantastical double life" within the family. If interrupted by members of the household while enacting it, they would pretend to be reciting memory work for school. So enthralling was this make-believe world that the two would steal off to pursue their game in private whenever they could. Caroline and Mazo were periodically separated, and the Play had a ritualistic role in their reunions, serving as a test of Caroline's loyalty and devotion.

When Caroline and Mazo had one of their rare failures of understanding after Mazo discovered her cousin holding the hand of an exotic young Latin neighbour in Parkdale, the cure for her sense of isolation and betrayal, as well as Caroline's despair at the young man's departure, was not long forthcoming. What could Mazo do to make Caroline smile again? Why, she could evoke the Play, decked in brighter colours, with new characters of both sexes and of all ages and stations of life. It would allow them to forget the disappointments of the summer. (This time, the two went overboard in their exuberance at the Play's revival, violently killing off one of their favourite characters, which upset them to the point of tears and sleeplessness; they were moved to resurrect this character the next day, allowing him to live out his years as a happy and flourishing farmer.)

Then, after Mazo suffered her nervous breakdown in 1903, the year after her first publication, the Play served as therapy. On returning from a sojourn on the shores of Georgian Bay, she was reunited with Caroline at a cottage the Roches had taken on Lake Simcoe. The play did not fail them; indeed, new characters erupted from Mazo's fertile brain. Now she was able to give to their speeches what she was, after her breakdown, unable to give to her writing, which was blocked. The play became more subtle, with both actors paying more attention to the craft of its telling; and if it was still a great strain on Mazo's nerves to write, quite the opposite was true when it came to creating the play: "My written stories were mere cups that were inadequate to contain the stream. The capacity of our Play was boundless."

As late as 1957, the importance of the Play was still evident. That year, Mazo received a letter of congratulations from her editor, Edward Weeks, on the manuscript of her penultimate novel, *Centenary at Jalna* (1958). In his letter Weeks linked her Whiteoaks novels to the Play: "You have a great talent as a literary dramatist, and the larger the cast grows the more you seem to enjoy it. This is, I suppose, the direct development of that secret play which you devised for Caroline." The year 1957 also saw the publication of Mazo's autobiography, and in it she pinpointed what she saw as the difference between her and Caroline's invention of playmates and the games of other children. *They didn't stop their play!* Indeed, the two women no longer *acted* the parts of their characters — they *were* their characters. In recounting her life after winning the *Atlantic Monthly* prize for *Jalna*, when she would have been approaching fifty, Mazo demonstrates no embarrassment in confiding to the reader that after the speeches and receptions she would happily return to her make-believe world. Her last words to Caroline before falling asleep each night were not about the excitement of their outer lives; they were the words of a character from the Play. One imagines the two in their last five summers together, lying in deck chairs outside their rented cottage at The Briars, on Jackson's Point. Watching the sun set over Lake Simcoe, they shed the worries they have accumulated through the years as the words of Blount drift over the quiet water: "*Come on!*"

"Something More than a Child"

CUE. FAST-FORWARD.

In 1910, "The Spirit of the Dance," one of six early short stories Mazo de la Roche set in the imaginary Quebec village of St. Loo, appeared in the *Canadian Magazine*. A curious tale, incorporating Gothic romance into a setting reminiscent of that found in Duncan Campbell Scott's French Canadian stories, it focuses on the physically deteriorating Monsieur Louis de Valleau, sustained only by his Stradivarius violin and his daughter, Gabrielle, who reminds de Valleau of his bittersweet union with *une danseuse* in Rome. De Valleau's housemaid and his doctor decide that his recovery depends upon his rescue from two things, his Stradivarius and himself. Madame Berthe and Doctor Girard are mistaken on the first score, for depriving de Valleau of the musical creativity that connects him to the vital forces of life probably only hastens his end. In the second matter, however, they are closer to the mark: the seigneur *does* need rescuing from his self-destructive desires.

Mazo's story may, on the surface, seem far removed from her own experience — it was published between the time her father gave up running a hotel in Acton and the family took up farming near Bronte. Yet it expresses a theme that finds fuller expression in her more mature writing: the conflict between spontaneity and creative energy and those forces that would deny instinct and artistic impulse. At the same time, it contains a subtext that challenges the myth of the Victorian home as safe harbour, a myth that *Ringing the Changes* so desperately tries — and then fails — to preserve.

This subtext centres on the disturbing relationship that de Valleau has with his daughter, whom he calls upon to dance in her nightdress whenever he becomes possessed by the Spirit of the Poplar (the call of nature expressed through his violin). Gabrielle, as she grows "into something more than a child," reminds de Valleau of her mother, who deserted him in Rome, and who has been as injurious to his well being, from Madame Berthe's point of view, as the "brown harlot" Stradivarius. Encoded into this narrative is a view of father-daughter love as an unhealthy emotional dependency.

One evening, for instance, as Gabrielle reads to her father from a volume of verse, de Valleau covers the page with his white fingers and draws her closer to him: " 'Shut the book sweetheart,' he said, 'shut the book and let us sit quiet for a while together.' So Gabrielle stretched her arm across his knees and laid her head against his breast with her face upturned to his; and the Seigneur looking down at her, praised the tinting in her cheeks and hair and said her mouth was like her mother's" (*Selected Stories*). Their relationship has some affinity with Mazo's memories of her bond with her father at the time she and her parents were living in Galt, when Mazo was entering adolescence:

> Often my father and I read the same book at the same time, his six foot three extended in an easy chair, my growing length draped against his chest. . . . I think it was in these days, when first we began to read together that the bond between my father and me strengthened into a deep understanding and we became the most loved of friends. As he waited for my slower grasp of the page to catch up to his, as his large shapely hand was raised to turn the page, a palpable emotion stirred within us. My love for my mother was instinctive. I took her devotion for granted. But he was my hero, my protector, my gay companion. . . . As I grew older and young men appeared on the scene I invariably compared them with him, to their disadvantage — till the day when one arrived who could better bear comparison with him. (*Ringing*)

Present-day readers cannot help but discern sexual stirrings in both passages, father to daughter and daughter to father. Gabrielle de Valleau belongs to the Cinderella legend, where the daughter's desirability to her father is strongly linked to her striking resemblance to her mother, whereas Mazo simply belongs to that legion of Victorian daughters who worshipped their Freudian papas. If, however, we've lost our innocence, we are certainly in a better position to understand Mazo's reticence in presenting certain aspects of her life story.

The household into which she was born, Grandpa Lundy's, had been the cauldron in which her mother's ill health, excitability, and highly emotional nature had been brought to a boil. According to Mazo, Alberta "seemed to bring out the worst" in Daniel Lundy, resulting for her in a childhood of "painful scenes." Although he got on well with his sons, being a "kind and indulgent father," and was always — or so the story goes — sweet to Caroline and Mazo, Daniel, from the beginning, found his eldest child to be a thorn in his side. Mazo tells us in the very first chapter of *Ringing the Changes* how her grandfather would force her mother to sit by his side when she incurred his displeasure and listen to hour-long lectures, during which "she would fairly tear herself to pieces with sobbing," her face "disfigured by the salt flow of her tears." These sessions were followed by corporal punishment.

As Louise DeSalvo has observed in her study of the impact of childhood abuse upon the writing of Virginia Woolf, in a patriarchal family (in contrast to William Roche's upbringing, Alberta Lundy's was regulated by paternal authority), sons enjoy privileges denied to daughters, whose activities are controlled and restricted by the patriarchal despot. That Daniel Lundy had a very different relationship with his sons is therefore not surprising. Like many Victorian women, Alberta exhibited behaviour that formed the usual stuff of case histories arising from such a background: depression, long-term psychosomatic illness, extreme nervousness, unfounded fears. Yet, to quote DeSalvo, "the real 'cases,' the genuine examples of psychopathology, could be found in the study of Victorian fathers."

Mazo tells us of the other side of Daniel Lundy's relationship with his daughter: "There were times when his love for my mother was roused and took an almost extravagant turn." As an adult, after one of her long illnesses, Alberta received from her father "a mass of greenery," which he had procured from the woods, in the belief that the aroma would have a salutary effect upon his daughter's "nervous breakdown." Afterward, Mazo remembers staring into the embowered sickroom at her "small and rather overpowered" mother. She also recollects her grandfather's fierce jealousy of his daughter Eva's suitors; he would demonstrate icy disapproval towards them, saving his verbal abuse until later, when he could unleash it upon his wife in their bedroom. Mazo and Caroline, in the adjoining room, would often overhear him. Yet this was the grandfather Mazo adored, devoting several pages of her autobiography to her extreme grief over his death.

Of course Mazo's early years weren't all spent in her grandfather's home. When she was only three, her father, having failed to make a go of his Montreal Tea House and Family Grocery, moved his family south to the neighbouring village of Aurora, where he became manager of The Leading House, an importing business owned by his older brother, Danford. Mazo and her parents went back to Newmarket when Danford moved to Toronto to establish a Yonge Street emporium that would compete with Timothy Eaton's. Mazo's father took over the Newmarket shop. When William decided it was all or nothing, and sold the stores in Newmarket and Aurora in order to direct all his energies to Danford's Yonge Street venture, he finally moved his family to Toronto, eventually settling in the Roche house on 113 John Street.

It must have been quite a contrast to the Lundy domicile. Now Mazo and her parents shared intimate quarters with Mazo's paternal grandmother and two uncles, as well as other members of the family. The cadences of the deep musical voices of her Roche relations, voices to which she awakened and fell asleep, would surface in her prose, just as the passionate natures of her pleasure-loving kin would later form the foundation of her characters' joie de vivre. And while the multigenerational makeup of Jalna can be traced not only to the Roches of John Street but also to the multitude of Lundys with whom Mazo's family later lived in Toronto, it is beyond doubt that the reckless abandon and high-spirited joy that unite the Whiteoaks uniquely reflect the Celtic influence of the tall, handsome Roches who loved so much to talk.

Still, Mazo's descriptions of several incidents from her early days suggest troubling undercurrents beneath the placid surface of her idealized childhood. The most striking of these is a powerful nightmare that she had when she was only eighteen months old. It occurred after she had experienced "trembling terror" at the sight of a feather blowing across the floor. In her nightmare, she found herself standing helplessly in "a dim tunnel" through which "an enormous ball" was rolling. The movement of this ball was accompanied by a "distant roaring sound" and "a strange smell, the very essence of evil."

On a more prosaic level, Mazo also recalls her parents' response to her first short story, which she had written, at the age of nine, with the aim of winning a contest. The tale of a lost child finally restored to her mother's arms, it prompted her own mother to doubt that a hungry child would eat potato parings and that her mother would quote a text from the Prodigal Son upon her return. Mazo's father, on the other hand, exclaimed, "I'm dead sure I'd eat potato parings if I were hungry enough," adding that the text "was the proper thing for the mother to quote. Don't change a word of [the story]. It will probably get the prize." It did not win the prize.

Alberta Roche again appears in the role of critic and pragmatist when, after a little boyfriend of Mazo's receives a rowing machine and a Bible for his birthday, Mazo asks for the same: " 'Neither of them,' she answered decisively, 'is suitable for a child!' " One questions whether she'd have objected to the rowing machine had Mazo been a boy; as for the Bible, one suspects her reasoning was following the same line it had some time later, when she halted a reading of *Othello* that she and her husband had begun for Mazo, recoiling at the play's overt sexuality. Immediately after this anecdote, incidently, Mazo remarks upon her cousin's appreciation of beautiful clothes, her love of sewing and shopping and planning a wardrobe. Clearly, Caroline's preferences were more compatible with Alberta Roche's. As for Mazo, she never longed to engage in such grown-up activities: "I wanted to remain a child secure in the shelter of my home."

Sandwiched between the years Mazo and her parents spent in the large Roche and Lundy households, the sites of Mazo's childhood and adolescence, is the time they spent in Galt (now Cambridge). Removing to rooms in the Queen's Hotel in the early 1890s so that Alberta might recover her health, the three must have enjoyed the privacy afforded by their own living quarters: this is the time of Mazo's growing intimacy with her father.

Galt was also the scene of Mazo's growing awareness of her gifts as a writer, of a spiritual awakening. Here occurred her Wordsworthian discovery of nature and its beauties as something separate from herself. Until this point, she had simply been part of the world, and unconscious of it. Her emotions had been instinctive; now, one spring morning in Galt, she stood in conscious wonder at the Creation. Echoing Wordsworth's "I wandered lonely as a cloud," she remarks, "I gazed and gazed. I felt that never should I again be the same." She gave up childish reading, began to see the sun as "a great red flower . . . throwing its petals of fire across the world." Ducks were no longer simply ducks, but appeared as actors in a play — the colours of the landscape seemed to have been invented for her alone. Thus were born those extravagant tropes that distinguish her writing.

About the same time Mazo's father presented her mother with a pug. The dog soon began to wear on Alberta's frazzled nerves, and was confined in a box room. In that room, Mazo, while looking after the animal, found a shabby old book on ancient and modern history. It included a chapter on Greek legends and mythology, and suddenly Mazo was "not in Galt," caring for a dog that her father had irresponsibly thrust upon the household, but "in Greece," in the company of Proteus and Psyche and Narcissus, of Hero and Leander. Feeling "the rapture of a convert," Mazo turned not to the religion of her Lundy ancestors but to paganism, "worshipping at the shrines of the bad old gods." She never lost this sense of rapture, writing of pagan and mythical themes in her short fiction (most notably "The Sacred Bullock") and also her novels, both within and without the Jalna chronicles.

Alberta Roche's health did not improve in Galt, and the family headed back to Toronto, this time to Grandpa Lundy's home at 157 Dunn Avenue in Parkdale, acquired in 1894. Mazo brought with her two important findings: a secret awareness that her communion with the natural world had marked her as somehow different from the rest, an anchorite of the heathen gods; and a passionate bond with her father that occasionally erupts in her writing with the intensity of Louis de Valleau's wild melody as it pierces the silence of the night.

To return to "The Spirit of the Dance": Madame Berthe tells Doctor Girard that she has seen Gabrielle, through the keyhole of the door to the seigneur's bedchamber, darting and crouching and spinning to her father's demonic playing "like one possessed." After the music, Madame Berthe reports, there was silence, which was broken by the father's injunction, "Promise me that you will forget this night." Gabrielle, who has overheard the housekeeper's gossip, retaliates by accusing her of making love to the doctor: "It is no use to deny. I caught you in the act." But Madame Berthe placates Gabrielle, and convinces her to sell her father's violin to the landlord of the local tavern in order to save the seigneur's life.

When one evening de Valleau calls for his violin — " 'I am not to be denied this time! You see the music is here,' touching his forehead 'and it must get out at the fingers or — confusion — confusion — madness...' " — Gabrielle races through the darkness and retrieves the Stradivarius. Then, slipping off her clothes, she appears at her father's door in her nightdress. At first de Valleau's music comes as a whisper. His daughter's "flexuous young body hung for a moment in suspense.... her white limbs bathed in moonlight." Then the melody grows wilder, and Gabrielle's movements become one with the poplar whose branches wave outside the window, one with the singing violin — they are as "abandoned" as those of "a bird that swings on a wind-blown bough." This is a "supreme moment" for Gabrielle and her father, whose eyes meet in rapture as the dance proceeds... and then slowly dies. De Valleau's soul has passed into the night. "It was ashes after fire."

It *is* a curious story. D.H. Lawrence wrote of Poe's tales, "So there you are. There is a limit to everything. There is a limit to love."

"A Very Fragile Sort of Woman"

Alberta Roche's health did not improve in the home of the Lundy paterfamilias; indeed, it worsened. She rid herself of the cough that had plagued her in Galt, but was now increasingly bedridden with digestive problems and nervous agitation. She became terrified of being left alone, requiring the presence of a man. When Mazo arrived home from school each day, she felt stifled by her mother's suffering presence; at night she was prohibited from playing the piano.

The Dunn Avenue household consisted of ten members: the Lundy grandparents, Mazo and her parents, Caroline, two uncles, one aunt, and, later, W.R. Roche's very Irish Uncle Bryan, who more than anyone else was able to assuage Alberta's anxieties. An occasion did arise, however, when all the men of the family had to be away from home at once, which caused Mazo herself to experience panic. She worried about what would happen if her mother were to become aware of the absence of male support: "It might mean the snapping of that slender cord that bound her to reason" (*Ringing*). Inspired by the knowledge that the familiar sounds made by Great-Uncle Bryan — his deep voice and musical laughter, as well as his creaking boots on the stairs — were what comforted her mother most (note that it was Alberta's *husband's* uncle, not a member of her own immediate family, who anchored this slender cord), Mazo decided that a little exercise in impersonation might be expedient. Several times a day, she would mount and descend the stairs in Uncle Bryan's boots, trembling with nervousness and laughter.

She confesses that she rather enjoyed playing the part of her great-uncle, wearing the boots of a man of the house. After a week, however, the men returned, and Mazo could relax in the sun (her metaphor) of her father's presence, while her mother basked in that of Uncle Bryan. Mazo's memory here turns from boots to skates, for she remembers how she gave up the pleasure of ice-skating to care for her mother. We again sense Mazo's attraction to the free and easy world of men, as opposed to the claustrophobic domestic prison.

Mazo's imitation of Uncle Bryan was not, incidentally, her only venture into cross-gender dress up. Later, when her parents lived on Jarvis Street, she attired her paternal grandmother in a suit of her father's, as well as his grey homburg. Whom should Grandma Sarah Bryan Roche resemble but her brother — Uncle Bryan! He, at any rate, was the person for whom W.R. Roche pretended to mistake his mother. When her identity was "revealed," the two fell into helpless laughter. It is difficult to imagine such a scene occurring among the Lundys on Dunn Avenue, and the fact that Alberta joined in the fun indicates the extent of her recovery from her nervous breakdown. As for Mazo, her penchant for donning men's clothing was eventually accommodated by changing fashion, for after the success of *Jalna*, when she and Caroline were vacationing in Gloucester, Massachusetts, each bought and delighted in wearing a pair of slacks. Caroline told Ronald Hambleton that her cousin wrote in trousers — an interesting gloss, perhaps, on the relation between Mazo's craft and her conception of herself; in *Mary Wakefield* (1949), Adeline Whiteoak reflects upon the suitability of men's apparel for honest labour, thinking how grand it would be to wear nothing more than a shirt and trousers, like the men in the fields.

The affinity between grandmothers Sarah Roche and Adeline Whiteoak is extended in *Whiteoak Brothers: Jalna — 1923* (1953) when Mazo has Dilly Warkworth (a distant cousin whom Aunt Augusta has brought over to Jalna from England) dress old Adeline in men's hunting clothes from the attic. In her autobiography, Mazo describes her costumed grandmother as being transformed into "a rather rakish-looking old gentleman-about-town"; in *Whiteoak Brothers*, Gran's hunting attire invests her with "an ancient, rakish elegance."

Clothing provides another connection between Mazo's life and her art. The Lundy family annually mourned Uncle Frank, who had died a terrible death. Every spring, Grandpa Daniel would air his dead son's suits and smoking jacket, which Mazo imagined still held the shape of his body (*Ringing*). The same ritual is enacted by Adeline in mourning the death of her husband, Captain Philip Whiteoak, in *Young Renny* (1935); in this most moving scene of the novel, Adeline also experiences the uncanny sensation, as she shakes and brushes his evening and riding clothes, smoking jacket, tweeds, and regimentals before hanging them on the line, that the captain's vigorous body still gives its shape to his apparel.

It was the shadow of Daniel Lundy's death, however, that darkened Mazo's life at the turn of the century; and while she mourned his passing, she also confessed in closing this chapter of her story that she now "felt very strong and capable, as though I were no longer a very young girl, almost as though I had the helm of the family ship in my hands and could guide it."

Uncle Danford's Yonge Street emporium was finally crushed by the Eaton juggernaut around the time Mazo and her parents travelled to Galt, causing the breakup of the John Street household. William, his wife, his daughter, and Caroline settled at 469 Jarvis

Street, close to the Masseys and next door to the historian George M. Wrong. (Years later, Mazo would draw on Wrong's *The Rise and Fall of New France* and *The Canadians* while writing her own history of Quebec.) Lacking the stamina, according to the family doctor, to attend the University of Toronto on a full-time basis, Mazo took classes at the Ontario School of Art, where she studied under George Agnew Reid, known for his paintings of rural Ontario life, which dealt with some of the themes and subjects Mazo addressed in her fiction.

It was at this time that she published her first story, "The Thief of St. Loo," and then her second, "The Son of a Miser," in *Munsey's Magazine*. Mazo was feeling "strong and full of power" — and then her world fell apart. After mailing what she considered to be her best story to a magazine, she experienced a "strange unease" while waiting for a response, and then learned that a stamp had been found on the floor of the post office just after she had posted her manuscript. On making this belated discovery, she was overcome by vertigo, feeling as though she were slipping into an abyss. Then, attending by herself a performance of the medieval English play *Everyman*, she experienced emotional suffering so acute that for years afterward she could not bear to hear the name of the play. These terrifying sensations culminated in a visit to St. Michael's Cathedral, where Mazo kneeled at each Station of the Cross. Joan Givner argues that the morality play exacerbated Mazo's guilt about her love for Caroline and her resistance to roles assigned by gender. Furthermore, Givner sees the trip to St. Michael's as an expression of Mazo's "distaste for the woman in herself and the women in her family," because following her observances at the cathedral, Mazo, in the throes of alienation, openly confronted her strongly Protestant family "as though to show that I no longer belonged to them" (*Ringing*). This act of defiance was followed by a complete collapse.

The effect of this nervous breakdown, encapsulated in the title of the autobiographical chapter that documents it, "Clipped Wings," was a growing dependency on those around her: "I had been rather an independent girl — somewhat too sure of myself, I fear, though I don't think anyone would have called me conceited. But now, like a child, I wanted to be told what to do. This desire to have decisions made for me has clung to me the rest of my life." Certainly this self-assessment is substantiated by the reminiscences Hambleton recorded of those who knew Mazo in later life. Many of these people touch upon her nervousness and oversensitivity, her anxiety in dealing with crowds and meeting everyday demands. Mrs. Richard Elmhurst, widow of Stephen Haggard, who played Finch in the play *Whiteoaks*, remembered Mazo as "highly, highly over-sensitive . . . one of the most highly sensitive people I think I've ever met. She had this *overheated* imagination." Another friend spoke of her as "a very fragile sort of woman . . . she seemed to fly away from social contact in the mass, in the raw." Others recalled her fears relating to such simple matters as ordering a taxicab.

Mazo directly confronts her collapse in *Ringing the Changes*, discussing it in detail. She describes her convalescence at George Reid's house on Indian Road, which her parents rented for two summers, and, later, her striking out on her own to a hotel at Pointe-au-Baril, on Georgian Bay. Yet she completely omits her family's subsequent move to Acton, where they lived, with Caroline, from 1905 to 1908. Here, again, Mazo's omissions may well represent the most important part of her story.

Mrs. K. Dills, a former longtime resident of Acton whose husband owned the *Acton Free Press*, told me that when *Ringing the Changes* appeared, Actonites looked forward to reading about the Roches' time there. Imagine their surprise to find that Mazo had jumped directly from her breakdown to her family's move to Bronte at the end of the decade! The most obvious explanation would seem to be that Mazo was reticent to admit that her father ran the Acton House, a hotel with a barroom; after all, in her previous chapters she avoids referring to W.R. Roche's other occupations, such as cigar salesman and cutter in the clothing department of his brother's store. If the characters Mazo created in her fiction are idealizations of her family, then the portraits of her family she created in her autobiography are idealizations, as well. Yet this explanation is perhaps too obvious.

"*Other parts, you know you'll never find,*" writes Timothy Findley. Clearly Mazo didn't *want* her readers to know about her life in Acton. At her death, Caroline, under orders, burned her cousin's diaries — how far back these went we'll never know — thus obliterating whatever parts of Mazo's life she chose to keep private.

And so the mystery in which the two had wrapped so much of their life together was preserved.

Still, Mazo left clues to this mystery behind — in her novels and stories. Only recently have literary critics realized that *Delight* is her Acton novel; Ronald Hambleton, for example, mistook its landscape for the farming country north of Newmarket, while George Hendrick accepted Mazo's claim that the novel grew out of stories told by the family's cook at Bronte. Mazo herself gaily tossed red herrings in the paths of even her close friends, suggesting that some of the material came from her experiences at Foxleigh Farm (Bronte), but that the fishmonger belonged to her time at Trail Cottage. He may well have done, but the hotels, the tanneries, the quarries — the very soul of the novel — belong to Acton.

At the end of *Delight*, the heroine, Delight Mainprize, is subjected to a ritualistic chastisement and ostracism by the local women. Her crime is being different from them, living in harmony with her instincts in violation of social conventions. Now, if you, as an autobiographer, were going to avenge yourself on a community for having scorned your virtue and talents, what might you do? *Write it out of existence*. And so Mazo did, having already encoded her disdain for Main Street in her fiction: to mention Acton directly would have allowed Acton to exist.

Upon Bronte, on the other hand, she lavished her attention, painstakingly recreating in her autobiography the halcyon days of farming on the shores of Lake Ontario. It is into this setting, where the fruit is ripening on the trees, that she introduces the element hitherto missing from *Ringing the Changes*, her own tale of romance: the handsome suitor. His name was Pierre Mansbendel, and his arrival in Mazo's story has the same fairy-tale aura as Caroline's. Mazo met Pierre while visiting her Aunt Eva's boardinghouse. "[S]tartlingly handsome," he spoke with a "charming foreign accent," and though his "arrogance stood out all over him," beneath it — as is the case with Charlotte Brontë's Rochester and Jane Austen's Darcy — was great sensitivity. When Mazo told her mother and Caroline about Pierre, they were eager to meet this delightful wooer, but her father "seemed not at all sure that he would like him." When Pierre finally visited the farm, however, W.R. Roche proved a good deal more gracious than Renny Whiteoak, who thrashes an overly zealous pursuer of *his* only daughter, threatening to break every bone in his body.

Mazo's mother found Pierre almost too handsome, exclaiming, "And am I expected . . . to get used to that dazzling beauty about the house?" His perfect teeth, his wavy, jet-black hair, his full and arrogantly curved lips, his amber eyes, his fair complexion — all this perfection was marred by only one defect, a Byronic lameness resulting from a childhood bout of polio. But Pierre was not really interested in Mazo's parents — he wanted only to be with Mazo, night and day.

Yet Mazo confides to the reader that although Pierre expected her to be "enthralled" with him as he tramped up and down the fields flying a kite, she was not "the sort of female who knows no boredom, no fatigue, so long as she can trail after the man she fancies." Indeed, Aunt Eva's sudden arrival at the farm was a relief, for Mazo was in the midst of writing a story and wanted time to herself. The distractions seemed to multiply, however. The deaths of both of Mazo's grandmothers, as well as a pedigree Holstein, a litter of pigs, two beloved geldings, the Yorkshire and Irish terriers — to say nothing of an acute attack of appendicitis that endangered Mazo's own life — fell between Pierre's first visit and his next, when, upon returning from New York, he surprised the family by announcing that a man should wed for convenience rather than love; a few months later he and the ubiquitous Aunt Eva were married.

That Aunt Eva — whose age Mazo exaggerated by about ten years to make her nuptials seem even more extraordinary — should have married Pierre ties in with Mazo's earlier discovery, on Dunn Avenue, of Eva Lundy putting her arms around W.R. Roche, only to be rebuked by him; though, as she claimed, she had scarcely understood this scenario, Mazo had experienced a feeling of triumph. Now the one man Mazo would have us believe could bear comparison with her father had been ensnared by the same woman who had disrupted Mazo's first intimacy with Caroline, and later threatened the Play. The author of *Ringing the Changes* did not need to look very far to find the ogress for her fairy tale.

Mazo's revenge, should we choose to see it as such, was to re-create her aunt in the formidable Mrs. Handsomebody of *Explorers of the Dawn*, and later in the sex-starved Amy Stroud of *Whiteoak Heritage*

(1940). In that instalment of the Whiteoak chronicles, she took from the Bronte chapter of her autobiography the death of Johnny, a much-loved chestnut gelding, and blamed it on the malicious Mrs. Stroud; the woman turns Renny Whiteoak's favourite horse, Launceton, out into the freezing cold in retaliation for Renny's spurning of her amorous advances.

That Aunt Eva so conveniently fit the role of villain-scapegoat absolved Mazo, of course, of responsibility in the handling of the handsome suitor. She had been assigned the role of the woman jilted in romance, and could now find solace, as Victorian ladies were wont to do, in the company of an intimate female companion. "[Y]ears later," she assures us, she and Pierre "discovered the strength and loyalty of [their] love" (*Ringing*). In the mean time, this affair of the heart was eclipsed by the greatest ordeal of her life: the death of W.R. Roche. Mazo's first novel, *Possession* (1923), paid homage to those years the family spent on the fruit farm by Lake Ontario, and it was wrought out of the grief she experienced after losing her hero, her protector, her gay companion.

But first she chose to write of childhood, and to settle a few scores. The year in which her father suffered an agonizing death — 1915 — was also the year "Buried Treasure," the first of the stories that would eventually comprise *Explorers of the Dawn*, was published.

"Alas, For the Whiskered Sex!"

Mazo's attitude towards her first book became dismissive in her later years: in 1952, she referred to her collection of ten stories as "highly sentimental," while in *Ringing the Changes* she confessed, "I could not to-day write one of them — not to save my life." Yet *Explorers of the Dawn* was extremely well received when it appeared in 1922, going into a fourth printing the following January and making the best-seller lists.

Christopher Morley, who brought Mazo's writing to the attention of publisher Alfred Knopf and wrote the foreword to the book, was quick to appreciate the merit of the stories, which today are not without charm. What makes them particularly interesting to the contemporary reader is their playful self-referentiality, to say nothing, in this age of cultural studies, of what they reveal as symbolic constructions.

Explorers of the Dawn is set in the grey cathedral town of Misthorpe, England, but there are numerous clues within the text that indicate Mazo was drawing upon her early childhood in the Newmarket area and her adolescence in Toronto, as well as her adult life in Acton and later Bronte. Some of these clues should appeal to the postmodern sensibility. Take, for example, the first story, "Buried Treasure," which originally appeared in the *Atlantic Monthly*. In it, the three boys who form the nucleus of the collection of stories — David, John, and Alexander Curzon (ten, nine, and six years of age respectively) — seek imaginative escape from the repressive household of their governess and guardian, Mrs. Handsomebody. The opportunity to free themselves from her tyranny — their kindly father has gone to South America to build bridges following the death of their mother — presents itself in the person of the eccentric Captain Pegg, an archaeologist who lives next door with his son and daughter-in-law. Pretending to be a pirate, Pegg diverts the boys by burying some of his artefacts under their guardian's planked backyard, and then providing a map that will lead them to the treasure trove. Enter Mrs. Handsomebody, as the boys unearth the booty.

Clue number one: a back garden in an English cathedral town would certainly not have been planked, yet old-timers in Acton remember that muddy backyards in that town were usually covered with wooden planks. (Morley, an American, picked up on this incongruity in his introduction; furthermore, some of the boys' expressions struck Morley as "cisatlantic.") We can simply attribute such gaffes to Mazo's unworldliness. What Mazo's readers would not have perceived, however, is the self-referential humour she expresses through Pegg. Regaling the boys with tales of his crew's Herculean efforts to pilfer an old Spanish galleon, he concludes by remarking that afterwards his men divided the spoils, "and some of them gave up pirating and settled down as *inn-keepers* and tradesmen" (emphasis added). Even after her cousin's death, Caroline Clement categorically denied that Mazo's father had ever been in the hotel business in Acton, yet Mazo didn't mind having a sly go at her father's innkeeping fraternity.

Clue number two: the English cathedral town is named Misthorpe. The setting of *Possession*, Mazo's first novel, which she was already at work on when *Explorers of the Dawn* was published, is a farm near a fishing village on the shores of a large lake. This village is called Mistwell. *Possession*'s Grimstone is a fictional representation of the fruit farm near Bronte where the Roches lived from 1911 to 1915, the period during which "Buried Treasure" was written. Bill Cudmore, a descendant of the family that lived next door to the Roches when they farmed near this fishing village on Lake Ontario, is the current keeper of Bronte's foghorn. He points out its importance: Bronte frequently "mists in" — hence Mistwell, and, by extension, Misthorpe. So Mazo's supposedly English setting connects not only to her family's time in Acton but also to the Roches' subsequent years in Bronte.

Correspondences between *Ringing the Changes* and *Explorers of the Dawn* abound. In *Mazo de la Roche of Jalna*, Ronald Hambleton claimed that Mazo's first book charted a "mapless world," but the terrain it covers is not geographical — what is being mapped is the author's childhood. For example, in her autobiography Mazo dredges up one of her earliest memories, the sight of a terrified dog running down the street with a tin can tied to its tail, much to the amusement of the boys responsible for this cruelty; in the fourth story of *Explorers of the Dawn*, "A Merry Interlude," the Curzon boys rescue a black Scottish terrier named Giftie (the Roches' Scottish terrier Bunty) from a bullet-headed lout who has tried to do the same thing. In *Ringing the Changes*, Mazo remembers the big red bananas peddled by an Italian fruit vendor named Salvator Polito; in one of the stories in *Explorers of the Dawn*, each boy is given a long red banana by an Italian — named Salvator. In her autobiography, Mazo remembers the day she and a fiery young companion named Leigh found themselves surrounded by a group of rough boys, and the way Leigh quickly dispersed them; in "Freedom," the boys venture far from Mrs. Handsomebody's domain into a street where they are beset by a gang of youths — David, the plucky first-person narrator of the stories, administers a quick and effective jab to the nose of one of these belligerents. In

Ringing the Changes, a stuffed white owl in Mazo's grandfather's house haunts the early pages; stuffed birds in glass cases clutter Mrs. Handsomebody's suffocating parlour.

Then there are the links between the emotional lives of the boys and Mazo. When, for instance, the Curzons feel threatened by their grim guardian, they retreat to their curtained four-poster bed, playing out roles as though they were Elizabethan actors — always male. Storytelling, like the Play, is hidden from the feminine adult world, for Mrs. Handsomebody, like Aunt Eva, is not to be trusted. And, on the very last page of Mazo's first book, her nine-year-old narrator, attending a pantomime with his brothers and newly returned father, thinks to himself that his own life, much of which is led in the imagination, is just as good as the play he's attending.

For whom were these stories written? Morley's foreword and the reviews of the day suggest an adult audience trying to recapture elusive childhood. The foreword compares the author to James M. Barrie and Kenneth Grahame. Today one cannot help but wonder how a woman could write what can only be described as a misogynistic fantasy about childhood, but in Mazo's day audiences addicted to Mark Twain (to whom Caroline was distantly related) and Booth Tarkington obviously revelled in seeing gutsy little boys outsmart grown women and conniving little girls.

An indication of how far this misogyny extends lies in the seventh story, "Granfa." The boys are taken fishing by their other neighbour, Bishop Torrance — another fun-loving emigré from the oppressive world of matronly authority. When little Alexander (also known as the Seraph) decides to free his bait, a worm called Charles Augustus, a dew worm he names Ernstine chases the male into the grass, wearing a predatory "cave-woman look." This occurrence is observed by Granfa, an "ancient rebel against authority" who has joined the fishing party in his flight from the workhouse. ("We pictured the workhouse as a vast schoolroom where white-haired paupers laboured over impossible tasks, superintended by a matron, cold and angular, like Mrs. Handsomebody.") Granfa shares the Seraph's view that his worm is doomed, assenting, "her'll get him and hold him fast too, I'll be bound. A terr'ble powerful worm."

Although set in Victorian times, these stories are fascinating in what they tell us about the narrative desires of an early-1920s North

American middlebrow audience. But while Mazo's representation of the sexes no doubt satisfied these desires and expressed commonly held and socially reinforced attitudes concerning gender, *Explorers of the Dawn* also seems curiously idiosyncratic; that is, there is so much in these stories that is already what we might want to call "Mazoian."

In an article entitled "My First Book," Mazo reflected upon her characterization in *Explorers of the Dawn*: "The small boys had no prototypes in real life. I wrote of them because, since my girlhood, I have had a great weakness for small boys. A small girl seems to me an embryo woman but a small boy is like nothing else on earth — a being apart." The same attitude is evident in the two books she wrote in the 1930s based upon her adoption, in England, of a boy and a girl. Even today, Esmée Rees, Mazo's adopted daughter, testifies to Mazo's blatant preference for males, manifested in her partiality to René, Esmée's adopted brother.

Although she claimed that the Curzon boys had no prototypes, their behaviour links them to Mazo's father (and his two brothers). For example, the lads drive Mrs. Handsomebody to distraction by sneaking a pregnant dog — and later an exotic bird — into her household. The reader of *Ringing the Changes* may recall that W.R. Roche brought an unwanted puppy to his ailing wife and overburdened daughter in their hotel suite in Galt. The Curzons' preoccupation with their own masculinity also ties them to Mazo's father, whom she frequently describes as an overgrown boy; in returning from a long business trip to British Columbia, he dazzles his womenfolk with an embroidered white buckskin hunting jacket given to him by a Native chief — a gift that symbolizes a small boy's dream vision of manly adventure.

Another passage in Mazo's autobiography illustrates what was, in fact, the matriarchal nature of the Roche-Bryan families. When W.R. and his older brother, Danford, were engaged in a game of billiards one Sunday afternoon, their mother abruptly put an end to their play by sternly reminding them it was the Sabbath: the two men, though in their fifties, hung up their cues "with shame-faced grins." It was their Grandmother Bryan, however, who was the real force to be reckoned with, for her dominating nature and hot temper "overbore her children and her children's children"; W.R. Roche and his brothers, who had to live without a father figure from a fairly young age, were guided by her — as the third generation of Whiteoak whelps were ruled by *their* grandmother — but by Mazo's account they were a handful. She affectionately portrays her father to the reader as a big, fun-loving boy, always forgiven his irresponsible actions because of his Hemingway-like joie de vivre.

In *Explorers of the Dawn*, David Curzon Sr. is another absentee father, and Mrs. Handsomebody frequently laments the boys' lack of discipline from a "strong man." When their handsome sire finally does return, he brings with him the influence of the healthy, liberating life he leads as a roving civil engineer. The sure force of his virility immediately pulls his sons into line, while allowing them the high jinks that are a normal part of boyhood.

Mazo clearly identified with the free-and-easy life she associated with little (and big) boys — her father, for instance, assigned her the name of a young warrior from one of H. Rider Haggard's adventure novels. The repressive (and repressed) roles belong to women. Mrs. Handsomebody, an embodiment of negative energy, administers chastisements and deprivations, and is always quick to put an end to joyful play and imaginative activity. True, her Irish servant, Mary Ellen, recognizes that the boys' pranks are "jist man-nature," and, unlike her employer, has no difficulty accounting for "the vagaries of the male"; yet her own healthy instincts are also subdued by her life-denying mistress, who is as narrow and towering as the façade of the house in which she lives.

The message of *Explorers of the Dawn* is succinctly expressed in several passages within the text. Shortly after David Curzon (otherwise known as Angel) expresses his view that girls are "the most sickenin' things," his brother John consoles himself with the thought that he's a boy. His experiences during his sojourn at Mrs. Handsomebody's have convinced him that women have to be "drowned out." After the boys' ogre of a guardian has ordered them to bed and confiscated Giftie's puppies, their misogyny reaches a new crescendo:

> Women! Tyrants! Mischievous busybodies!
> "When I'm a man," said Angel, suddenly, "I'll marry a woman, and I'll beat her every day."

"Me too!" cried The Seraph, stoutly, "I'll mawy two — fat ones — an' beat 'em bofe."

John simply opts for "unhampered bachelorhood," though he is comforted by his brothers' fantasies of having women in their grip.

For all their imaginings, the cold fact is that the boys are in the helpless grip of Mrs. Handsomebody, who can browbeat almost any man into submission, except for Father, the hero of John's dreams. After witnessing the "Dragon's" humiliation of the local cobbler, young John laments, "Alas, for the whiskered sex!" Curiously, in the autobiographical *The Very House*, written in the next decade, Mazo portrays herself as repeatedly exclaiming, "Bless my whiskers!"

We should not be too quick to infer from Mazo's treatment of the sexes that her attitudes were entirely representative of her culture. Prior to Caroline's arrival, Mazo was an only child isolated within large households of mature family relations. Furthermore, as the daughter of a frequently bedridden, neurotic mother, Mazo was conditioned by an environment that must have been deeply affected by her father's pronounced masculinity and the freedom, healthiness, and good fun it represented. Still, the Lundys and Roches were by no means divorced from cultural attitudes that celebrated the masculine by devaluing and ridiculing the feminine.

Significantly, *Explorers of the Dawn* is dedicated to Mazo's mother, who had laughed with her daughter over *"the adventures of these little fellows."* Mazo had to have been grieving over the recent death of Alberta Roche, and yet the Curzon boys, whose mother has been in her grave for a mere two months, demonstrate only a longing for their father's manly presence. When we confront the self-denial that results from meeting the expectations of those we love, we begin to grieve. Mazo grieved for her mother, but did she grieve for herself? In spite of the joy and love and childish wonder that lure us into this treasury of stories, buried within it is a terrible sense of betrayal.

Possession

When David Curzon Sr. arrives from South America at the end of *Explorers of the Dawn* and liberates his three boys from their captivity at Mrs. Handsomebody's, his son John desperately clings to Curzon Sr., exulting in the "all-surrounding power and protection of him." Yet, after travelling with his family to a pantomime in a hansom cab, John describes being physically close to his father in terms that convey a disturbing duality: the manly Victorian papa's leg and boot cruelly press against his offspring, producing both pain and "a delicious sense of protection and good fellowship."

To read *Ringing the Changes* in concert with Mazo de la Roche's fiction is to discover the extent to which the author inscribed her life — not only the conflicts of her inner world but also the physical details of her outer world — into her narratives. The relation between these two spheres is revealed in *Possession*, which was conceived in a flat above a launch house on Lake Joseph, Muskoka, to which Mazo and Caroline retreated shortly after the death of Alberta Roche. Although Mazo dedicated *Possession* to Christopher Morley, waiting until she wrote *Jalna* to dedicate a book to the memory of her father, it is not her mother's but her father's death that haunts the pages of her first novel. And while the father figure in this narrative, William Jerrold, is another protective playmate to his child — a girl this time, named Grace — his influence upon her might well remind one of the painful pressure of John Curzon's leg and boot.

Mazo wrote in her autobiography of *Possession* that "The scene of it was to be our farm on the lakeshore. That bit of land, the Indian fruit-pickers I knew so well, were to be pictured in it." Her active imagination was fervently unleashed one evening when memories of Rochedale (Foxleigh Farm), where the Roches lived from 1911 to 1915, surfaced, prompted by the sound of the boats gently rocking on the rough lake below.

When *Possession* was published in 1923, Mazo communicated to William Arthur Deacon, literary editor of *Saturday Night*, the emotions that had gone into its making: "I have tried with all the power that is in me to depict the life on this farm, in the warm belt of Western Ontario, where on a fine day the spray of Niagara is visible. . . . Some of the happiest, and by far the most tragic years of my life were spent there, so that I have a sort of passionate sensitiveness about the book that you may understand" (qtd. in Givner). From the time of the Roches' arrival, this life revolved around the comings and goings of livestock, including the death of a beloved horse and the particularly gruesome killing of a family dog by farmhands, who mistakenly thought it had rabies. Both events eventually found expression in the Jalna novels. To this was added an increasing financial strain, aggravated by W.R. Roche's frequent absences from the farm, during which the three women were left alone to cope with all the responsibilities. But the tragedy to which Mazo referred was unquestionably the diagnosis in late 1914 of her father's terminal illness, which put to an abrupt end these happy — and trying — years.

The fidelity of Mazo's re-creation of the setting was a tribute not only to her father but also to their seventy-two-acre farm, the woodland and fields and lake. The parallels between it and Grimstone, the farmhouse in *Possession*, are striking. Grimstone is also a century old, less than one hundred feet from the water, surrounded by towering elm locusts, near a fishing village. Grimstone, too, has a flagged yard, apple house, large orchard adjoining berry beds, and a poultry barn sheltering turkey hens, leghorns, and white Wyandottes.

Even more significant is the imaginative influence that the farm's lakefront setting had upon Mazo. Thirty-two years after *Possession*'s publication, she would tell interviewer Ronald Hambleton, "that lake, darkling in the summer moonlight, wild in the wintry storms, has meant as much to me as does the land." As already noted, throughout Mazo's writing the lake stands as a powerful symbol of freedom, a source of life, its rhythms expressing the vital force that pulsates within and without humankind. In describing its liberating influence upon her characters, and their instinctive attraction to water, she produced some of her most original writing, and her innermost longings are perhaps more clearly revealed in these descriptions than anywhere else. So, while Rochedale provided the immediate setting for only one novel, it can be argued that it was, in fact, the most singular influence upon all her fiction. Drawing upon the spiritual energy imparted to her by Lake Ontario,

Mazo articulated her central theme: the war between instinct and convention.

Possession's characters embody this struggle. The hero, Derek Vale, "frequently the subject of unexpected impulses," is locked in battle with the Chards, his stodgy neighbours, as well as a dour housekeeper, meddling clergymen, and even a noisy mob. A manly young architect from Halifax who inherits his uncle's farm, Derek finds that Grimstone brings out his strongest instinct, the desire to protect. Yet life becomes a muddle when this instinct leads him to shelter a seventeen-year-old Native woman, Fawnie, whose illegitimate baby boy testifies to Derek's unregulated sexual impulses.

Mazo's blond-haired, blue-eyed hero courts the fair-haired Pure Maiden of Romance, Grace Jerrold, and manages to walk the straight and narrow, with only a few side steps, until one summer evening. The first of a fairly long line of voyeurs in Mazo's novels — Derek is "unable to resist dark-eyed little girls" — he sees that night a party of Native berry pickers cavorting in the lake. The naked bathers, illuminated by "Ruddy tongues lick[ing] about a heap of driftwood," include Fawnie, rising from the waves like "a dark water-lily on its stem." When Derek's heart gives a "sudden leap," sending hot thrills of pleasure, like pain, through his body, his fate is sealed.

This is pretty heady writing for a Canadian novel of the 1920s, though when Fawnie arrives at Grimstone with her baby the reader is almost as surprised as Derek, for sex — and here, again, Mazo was setting the pattern for all of her fiction — is only hinted at through low murmers and giddy kissing. Mazo was also relatively daring in her presentation of *Possession*'s love triangle. The archetypal pattern is that the faceless hero is tempted by the dark-haired, sensuous lady, but renounces his desire in favour of the Pure Maiden; however, Mazo undermines this outcome by having Derek marry Fawnie, renouncing his love for Grace.

In *Possession*, Mazo sides with those characters who express the vitality of nature. Derek is drawn to Fawnie because she is the "completest human being he had ever known"; she instils in him a Lawrentian "intense consciousness of the earth"; she is "mother of him and of all thriving, air-sucking things." Like William Jerrold, Grace's father, Derek has never lost his boyish love of life, and the bond between the two men is strengthened by the great pleasure they taken in their own bodies.

Yet the realist in Mazo denies *Possession* a happy ending. Little Buckskin, the result of Derek and Fawnie's premarital passion, dies of a seizure, and the last page of the novel finds Grace Jerrold on a bluff overlooking Grimstone as the man she loves lies with the mother of his child. And herein can be found perhaps the most autobiographical aspect of the novel, Grace's frustrated passion for Derek and intense love for her father, with whom she remains.

Mazo's descriptions of William Jerrold greatly resemble those of her own father in *Ringing the Changes*. Both are lovers of purebred animals; they wear rough tweed coats, have finely moulded mouths, and gaze at their daughters with large dark eyes. Grace cannot stay away from her father, we are told — she loves him too much: "There's just the two of them. Always together." And, like W.R. Roche, the large and handsome William Jerrold, whose business head is not equal to his daughter's, faces economic ruin. He is obliged to hold an auction, which closely resembles the auction Mazo describes in her autobiography, the one her family held when forced to leave Rochedale. A fictional soulmate to Mazo, who writes in her autobiography of playing cards with her dying father in a dingy house in Oakville after moving from the farm, Grace is left to play cribbage with William Jerrold.

Mazo would go on to create happy endings, but her "passionate sensitiveness" about *Possession* was interwoven with memories of her own stricken hero and protector staring out the window at the cold grey lake. In her next novel, *Delight*, she would focus on her earlier days in Acton, but also travel beyond the sexual cul-de-sac of Freudian fathers and male suitors. *Delight* is a paean to female beauty, a celebration (though sometimes a covert one) of the delights of female sexuality.

★ ★ ★

27 JULY 1994

I came a little nearer to Mazo tonight, speaking to Mrs. Marjorie Tyrrell, the only one of the eight "tow-haired" Cudmores — the

Chards, in *Possession* — still alive. She is eighty-four years old, the youngest of the blue-eyed children who lived next door to the Roches when Mazo's family farmed on the shores of Lake Ontario, near the fishing village of Bronte. She doesn't know why Mazo treated the Cudmores so unkindly in her novel. And she insists that her siblings did not have "broad pasty faces" of which "the nostrils seemed the only noticeable feature": they were quite physically attractive.

Her nephews Bill and Jack told me Mazo stories handed down to them by their fathers and aunts and uncles, stories that had already been passed on to Ronald Hambleton. But here, I realized as I spoke to Mrs. Tyrrell, was an actual voice from the time the Roches lived at "the old Crabbe farm"; here was the child laughing at W.R. Roche as he floated on his back in Lake Ontario, a book propped on his stomach. The Cudmores were so astonished they called Mazo's father "W.R. Book." The image of this portly man bobbing among the waves contrasts wildly with the portrait of the handsome Victorian papa in Mazo's autobiography. I heard a new story, too. The Roches, Mrs. Tyrrell feels, looked down upon the Cudmores as "local-yokels." (And the Roches were *terrible* farmers, according to the Cudmores.) So you can imagine their delight the day a goat butted Mazo over the wire fence separating the two properties.

Did Mrs. Tyrrell remember Major E.F. Osler, reputed to be the model for *Possession*'s William Jerrold? Oh yes, the Cudmores' recently acquired Airedale — his name was Tubby — killed some of Osler's sheep, and Osler demanded that he be destroyed. The major held Christmas parties for the local children every year — at the church in Bronte? — and presented them with delicious oranges. (Even after losing his house and wealth, Jerrold still distributes oranges at these Christmas celebrations.)

And did Mrs. Tyrrell recall the little graveyard that Mazo situated just east of Grimstone, the century-old stone farmhouse of the novel? Oh yes, it's likely still there, though both the Cudmore and Crabbe houses have given way to an expensive housing development, and a good deal of the shoreline has eroded: there used to be "some pretty gruesome tales of caskets washing away." No stone house, though: her family's farmhouse was white strap and batten, and she remembers the Crabbe house, Rochedale to Mazo's family, as red brick. (In 1988, the town of Oakville moved the house to a site further east along the shoreline, where it is being restored.)

Finally, what about the Native berry pickers? Well, there actually was a funeral, like the one in the novel, on the Chard property. The father of one of the Native women who worked for the Cudmores had walked all the way from the reserve at Brantford, only to drop dead upon arrival. Was the old man a chief, a direct descendant of Tecumseh, like Fawnie's father in *Possession*? Mrs. Tyrrell can't recall. It was a long time ago. She was just a baby when the Roches were her neighbours. She doesn't remember much more — it has been eighty years. I thank her, and think of the goat butting Mazo over the fence . . . and smile.

Delight

Delight draws upon the period 1905 to 1908, when W.R. Roche was proprietor of Acton House and the family lived across the way on Main Street. Mazo did not begin the novel, however, until she and Caroline were summering at Trail Cottage, Clarkson, in 1924; in fact, *Delight* was published only a year before *Jalna* won the famous ten-thousand-dollar *Atlantic Monthly* competition.

The physical setting of *Delight* bears a remarkable resemblance to Acton and its surroundings — the hotels, the large tannery, the glove factories, the park with a racecourse bordering on a millpond (today Acton's Fairy Lake), the nearby quarries, the lonely grey-stone farmhouses squatting in the folds of the hills. This picturesque if somewhat desolate landscape of rocks and hemlock remains — one can view it from the train heading east towards Georgetown from Guelph — though W.R. Roche's Acton House long ago met a fiery end.

Yet in creating a locale for *Delight*, de la Roche incorporated Acton and its inland countryside, extending some twenty miles north of Bronte, into the lakefront setting she had used in *Possession*. The Duke of York, in which *Delight* opens, strongly suggests W.R. Roche's Acton House, yet Mazo situates the hotel, with its rough boarders and drinking rooms, in the town of Brancepeth, on the same lakeside road that passes through Mistwell. Just as Brancepeth is mentioned in *Possession* — Derek Vale attends church there — in *Delight* there is mention of Mistwell and Stead, to which have been rather incongruously added (to those familiar with this part of southern Ontario) Northwood, Stebbing, and Mertonbrook, hamlets along the quarry road.

Literary license? Of course. And, as is often the case with Mazo's obfuscations, keeping the identity of Acton a secret seems on one level simply a game. Indeed, *Delight* includes one character, borrowed from the earlier Acton-inspired short story "Canadian Ida and English Nell," who makes deception into an art. In using a false name, pretending to be her husband's cousin, and deducting a decade from her age, May Phillips discovers the delights of playacting, of "fool[ing] everybody." Note the parallel with Mazo, who altered her surname, referred to Caroline as her sister, and deducted nine years from her life.

Yet Mazo's smoke screens involved much more than a sense of play. Lovingly dedicated to Caroline, the novel abounds in richly varied sexual symbolism, centred on Delight Mainprize. For example, the heroine begs her beau, Jimmy Sykes, to pierce her ear, but he cannot meet this "unexpected demand on his skill, his courage, and his manhood." He is overcome by the intimacy of Delight's fervent request that he put a hole through her earlobe. Jimmy is then humiliated by the virile Duncan Kirke, who does the job "with pitiless precision." Later, on a roundabout with Delight at the fall fair, Kirke repeatedly thrusts a dagger through a golden ring in order to win free rides. A crowd gathers to witness his prowess, as the dazzling Delight grows dizzier and dizzier.

Linking her sex goddess to a number of archetypes of female sexuality — such as Diana, Eve, and Jezebel — and power — Delilah and Atropos, eldest of the three Fates — Mazo puts Delight through her paces not only in overheated hostelries filled with beer-swilling, beefy, and brawny men, but also on a lonely farm, where a demented religious fanatic plots to marry her off to a lascivious farmhand whose grotesque nature anticipates that of certain Alice Munro characters. Although the novel falls within the tradition of realism, its classical allusions and dramatic scenes invest it with a larger-than-life power, and at times the narrative seems to belong to the genre of the folktale — it is mythical rather than realistic.

While it is clearly feminine beauty that the novel celebrates, its comic ending confirming that all is right with the world when the devoted Jimmy Sykes finally wins Delight's hand, there are disturbing scenes as well, unsettling enough to have caused some critics to fault the novel for tonal inconsistency. Its darker conflicts arise, once again, in the battle between instinct and convention.

Like Fawnie in *Possession*, Delight Mainprize embodies the instinctive life. A natural child born out of wedlock to a chorus girl and a Russian ballet dancer, she comes to Canada an unsullied English country girl who has been living with her grandmother. Mazo's pagan divinity is all but buried under an avalanche of tropes linking her to the animal and vegetable worlds. Her mouth is "pink as a pigeon's feet"; her rising and falling breasts lay "like sleeping flowers between her rounded arms"; her shining golden hair "springs from the roots with strong vitality" — and, most tellingly, she is presented as "a creature of instincts, emotions, not much more developed intellectually than the soft-eyed Jersey in the byre." (In *The Bush Garden*, Northrop Frye observed that "It must be very rarely that a . . . wideawake and astute novelist . . . can call her heroine a cow with such affection, even admiration.")

The most important pattern of imagery, however, involves the crows that haunt the park, for while the rest of the town shoots them, Jimmy and Delight identify with these "savage wild things." As Desmond Pacey pointed out in his introduction to the New Canadian Library edition of the novel, the wild crows, "symbols of freedom, instinct, passion, and the primitive," are not only equivalent to Delight, but also appear in conjunction with the three crises of the narrative: when Jimmy takes a late-night walk with Delight after she dominates the dance floor at the Fireman's Ball; when Delight is unjustly accused of sexual misconduct by Miss Jessop, housekeeper at the Duke of York; and when Delight is attacked at the lagoon by a frenzied mob of women.

Delight's vital, instinctive nature, and, of course, her physical beauty, are what captivate the men of Brancepeth, but, with a few exceptions, they are also what antagonize her own sex. The final chapter of the novel contains one of the most forceful, if melodramatic, scenes in de la Roche's fiction. Delight is lured to the park by Mrs. Jessop, where she is assaulted by the housekeeper and her female accomplices; as they duck Delight in the lagoon, their faces are transformed by the molten sunset into "strange burning masks."

Derek Vale is subjected to a charivari, his community's response to his interracial, premarital sexual relations with Fawnie, and Delight, in turn, is attacked because of her sexual difference — her perceived looseness — that is, her vitality. Her sin is the simple animal joy she takes in life. In both Derek's and Delight's ostracism there is a ritualistic quality, accentuated by the electric torch that illuminates the hecklers in *Possession*, and the sunset that is reflected in the "burning masks" in *Delight*. These scenes can be interpreted as dramatizations of Mazo's own anxieties, of her feelings of marginality.

Yet *Delight* is arguably the most exuberant and unfettered of all Mazo's fictions. Possibly, as Dorothy Livesay has suggested, and as Timothy Findley has implied, Mazo's real power as a novelist rested in her ability to present, in Livesay's words, "the way ordinary people really lived, worked, loved, and hated" ("Remembering Mazo"). Certainly the one-act plays she wrote during the same period — *Low Life* (1925), *Come True* (1927), and the less successful *The Return of the Emigrant* (1929) — demonstrate the same ability to enter into the lives of ordinary people through a colourful use of dialect, an earthy humour, and a compassionate understanding of human frailties. Mazo would not return to this type of realism until 1938, when she wrote *Growth of a Man*, and while no Jalna-ite would have had it otherwise, one cannot help wondering what Mazo de la Roche might have written had she continued in this line of development.

★ ★ ★

25 AUGUST 1994

A day of contrasts. It begins with a visit to the Mississauga Golf and Country Club, where I am to meet Mazo's adopted daughter, Mrs. Esmée Rees. The club is located just north of the Queen Elizabeth

FIGURE 4

Originally a millpond powering a flour mill, Acton's Fairy Lake was given its name by Sarah Secord.

Way, in the heart of Whiteoak country, and is housed in a sprawling pseudo-Tudor structure with impressive views of the rustic-looking course, a palimpsest of late-twentieth-century leisure grounds that blanket an ancient burial site; the mounds are still visible. The Credit River, meandering through the valley below, was named for the transactions that took place between indigenous and European Canadians. The year before my visit, the club was invaded by an armed contingent of the dispossessed, protesting the desecration of their holy ground.

It's only later that I ponder how Mazo would have reacted to such a demonstration, let alone my edging my dirty farm truck next to a vintage Rolls Royce in the parking lot. Mind you, W.R. Roche and Renny Whiteoak didn't care for cars in the first place, but if we view these two vehicles as signifiers, which would Mazo choose? The one full of hay and covered with the dust of country roads, or the other, with its personalized license plates, shining in the August sun?

If Mazo de la Roche of Forest Hill represented the world of privilege, Maisie Roche of Newmarket and Acton was born into a very different world, one of constant struggle and frustrated ambition. I expect Esmée Rees, educated in private institutions and, later, at a Swiss finishing school, to embody the former way of life, yet my hosts introduce me to a disarmingly forthright and down-to-earth woman, certainly not without the signs of good breeding, but at the same time a no-nonsense sort of person on the lookout for pretense.

Describing herself as the "black sheep" of the family, Mrs. Rees recalls her adoptive mother displaying a chameleon nature at social gatherings and being a poseur in her dealings with men. There is, mind you, no disloyalty in Esmée Rees's description of her mother — only a forthright honesty. Simply put, the two women did not have a great deal in common. Esmée is quick to point out that she does not regard her mother's role-playing as having been false — we all play roles, she remarks, depending upon our company and circumstances. Still, it is clear that Esmée chose not to play the role her mother assigned to her.

Rather haunted by this conversation, and feeling more than ever that I will never really understand Mazo de la Roche, I head north to Acton, where I have arranged for further interviews. No ritzy parking lots here — instead a retirement home overlooking a lake, originally the millpond that Mazo's imagination transformed into the lonely lagoon where Delight Mainprize was set upon by the howling mob.

Finally Mazo comes into focus. She hadn't when my research directed me to *Acton's Early Days*, a collection of articles from the town's weekly newspaper published early in this century. Here I found references to her attendance at a church fund-raiser, to the Misses Roche riding about in a two-wheeled cart pulled by a Shetland pony. This was the official view. Now, standing in an overheated hallway listening to the gossip of one of the town's old-timers, I cross into another world, the seamy side of *Delight*.

Mazo, I am told, wasn't considered of much consequence in Acton. She had the reputation of being an "oddball, even at that time in her life"; she was a "bit weird." When the roads were being paved she would dabble her bare feet in the tar. She used to hang around the drugstore, reading the books on the shelves. "She was *always* Maisie Roche" in those days. (Indeed, when her father's purchase of Clark House was reported in the local paper, his name was ignominiously spelled "Roach.")

I speak to some other Acton residents. These people hold Mazo's reputation in higher repute, and I hear stories of the Beardmores, Acton's leading family. They would occasionally open the gates of their home, named Beverley — rather, I imagine, like the Criches do in Lawrence's *Women in Love* — to the townspeople. On such occasions the Roches likely conversed with Miss Hardy, the Beardmore children's governess, "very English" in her tweeds and brogues; the nannies; the frightening Mr. Pargeter, full-time gardener. After the Beardmores departed for Toronto, Beverley's lawn-bowling green was paved over and used as a parking lot, and Acton began its steady decline.

No wonder Maisie Roche haunted the drugstore looking for books and sought the solitude of the millpond! Yes, only two years after Sinclair Lewis escaped from Main Street, Sauk Centre, Minnesota, Maisie Roche moved to Main Street, Acton, Ontario. What pettiness, what meanness, the innkeeper's dreamy daughter must have experienced at the hands of the local gossips! Should we really be surprised that Caroline seems to have convinced herself that W.R. Roche never ran a hotel in Acton, or that in her autobiography Mazo completely omitted this part of her life, which conflicted so glaringly with her later conception of herself? Did Jimmy Gatz, once he became Jay Gatsby, believe in *his* former life?

Mazo clearly decided that the common people living outside Beverley's gates were not her sort — or the sort she had become. She might have identified with the life represented by my farm truck, but I suspect she wouldn't have approved of my parking it next to a Rolls Royce. Everything in its place.

Transition

If *Delight* comes out of the years the Roches spent in Acton, and *Possession* their time near Bronte, the autobiographical *Portrait of a Dog*, published in 1930, provides the bridge between the family's final days at Rochedale and the success of *Jalna* in 1927. Ostensibly the story of Bunty, the Scottish terrier Mazo presented to her dying father on his last Christmas as the Roches prepared to leave their farm, *Portrait of a Dog* is, as Mazo claimed, "also a shadowy portrait of my family" (qtd. in Hambleton, *Mazo de la Roche*).

Dedicated to "the other one," Mazo's designation for Caroline in the narrative, it addresses Bunty in the second person, referring to "your master" and "the one with the dark-blue eyes" (Alberta Roche). It carries us through the deaths of Mazo's father and, five years later, her mother; Mazo's emergence as a professional writer; summers at Lake Simcoe followed by winters in Toronto; and the palmy days at Trail Cottage near Clarkson.

Because Mazo speaks to Bunty directly, the reader feels part of this world; one is drawn into the warp and woof of the Roches' daily lives, their joys and sorrows. Resembling the weaver of many-coloured fabrics whose gently humming loom, in the flat above Mazo and Caroline's in Toronto, created a wall of peace against the outside world, Bunty's chronicler interweaves the past and present in a tapestry of words.

After the breakup of Rochedale, Bunty's family finds itself in Oakville, living in a divided dwelling. The details of this arrangement Mazo used when writing *Whiteoak Heritage* and *A Boy in the House* decades later. The dominant figure in this part of *Portrait of a Dog* is the dying master, who loves horses and is indifferent to cars; he has a "courageous masculine presence." Mazo's preoccupation with dichotomies in gender continues as the women of the family purchase another puppy, a West Highland terrier, when they move to the city after the master's death. In contrasting Bunty, a bitch, to Hamish, a male, the narrator presents Bunty as showing endurance and adaptability. Hamish is more wistful and flighty, "pathetically masculine." He represents the shadow side of the courageous masculine presence: in the realm of Scottish and West Highland white terriers, Mazo could comfortably ally herself with the female.

Bunty also outlives Hamish, who, like several animals in the narrative, falls victim to a car. Here the animal world is portrayed as one ruled by instinct, and always conflicts with the world of man and machines. Though nearly ten of Bunty's thirteen years are spent in blindness, she navigates through city street and country field by training her other senses; her courage and nobility stand out in these years of darkness. Of a time when dog and mistress find themselves in New York and miserable — this would be at Aunt Eva and Pierre's house — the narrator reflects, "Cities were not for you or for me. They could quench the thirst of the spirit no more than the sea could quench the thirst of the throat."

Their spirits *were* quenched at Lake Simcoe and later Trail Cottage, under whose roof the narrator found the tranquillity essential to her writing. And it was in the southern Ontario countryside that Bunty, who died at Christmas in 1927 in Toronto, was laid to rest, close to the cottage. Bunty's death closed, as the narrator of *Portrait of a Dog* maintains, a chapter of her family's life. Mazo was now a famous prize-winning novelist, Maisie Roche of Acton somewhere back in that vast obscurity beyond the city. Yet would she ever again be as happy as she had been in what, after Mazo's own death, Caroline Clement fondly remembered as that "ridiculous little cottage" not far from a house called Benares, with Bunty at her side?

Trail Cottage

In the summer of 1922, Caroline Clement stayed at the Blue Dragon Inn in Clarkson, a place fondly remembered by old-timers as having been as lovely as its name. This guest house was run by Margaret Fairbairn, whose daughter Grace evidently introduced Miss Clement to J.F.B. (Fred) and Florence Livesay. Fred was general manager of Canadian Press, his wife a journalist, translator, and writer of verse. Their young daughter Dorothy would blossom into one of Canada's finest poets and record poignant memories of Mazo de la Roche, a romantic figure to the local children.

The Livesays had just built a house, Woodlot, on what was originally part of Benares, the handsome estate of one of the area's most distinguished families, the Harrises. Annie (Harris) Sayers and her husband, Beverley, hoped to "form an agreeable neighbourhood" by selling building lots to suitable people (*Ringing*). When Mazo returned from Nova Scotia, where she had been sent to write a travel brochure on the Maritime provinces, she and Caroline decided that they could afford to buy two of the lots, which were being sold at modest prices. Mazo recalled in her article "My First Book" that sales of *Explorers of the Dawn* enabled her to build a summer cottage there.

They paid $1,400 for the two lots, and had Beverley Sayers engage a carpenter and obtain the services of a gardener-cum-woodcutter and a cleaning lady. Caroline and Mazo moved into Trail Cottage in May 1924, and were visited on their very first evening by Sayers who, in recognition of their maidenly seclusion, "strode to our doorway, bringing a handsome inlaid pistol to lend us." He must have shared the two women's sense of drama — Dorothy Livesay has confessed that she never understood why Mazo described the cottage as isolated, because the Livesays were within shouting distance.

Beverley Sayers's gesture reminds us, at any rate, of the genteel mode of living embraced by Mazo and Caroline's adoptive community. Mazo always denied that her fictional Whiteoaks were based on an actual family, though on certain points they resemble her own; however, the Whiteoaks dovetail with the Harrises, Sayers, Livesays, and other nearby residents when it comes to what they represent.

FIGURE 5

Mazo in communion with Trail Cottage in the 1920s.

In writing in her autobiography of the first of her sixteen chronicles of the Whiteoaks, she remarked, "*Jalna* was inspired by the traditions of that part of Southern Ontario on the fringe of which we had built Trail Cottage. The descendants of the retired military and naval officers who had settled there stoutly clung to British traditions." In this respect, her neighbours must have seemed the apotheosis of her Loyalist vision. Mazo was welcomed at the big house, with its spacious grounds, family portraits, and sense of the past. In this milieu, she met people with blue-blooded ancestry: Beverley Sayers's great-grandfather was William Henry Draper, "the first colonial statesman who could correctly be styled prime minister or premier in the whole history of the British empire-commonwealth . . ."; Draper was also Canada's first Supreme Court chief justice of the common pleas and "harbinger of the modern Conservative party in Ontario and Canada (Metcalf). On the other side of the family tree there was Captain James Beveridge Harris, justice of the peace and patriarch of Benares.

Annemarie Hagan, coordinator of the project, undertaken in the 1990s, to restore Benares and construct its interpretative centre, is quick to point out that the Harrises were anything but effete leisure-class snobs. They plowed their own land and produced their own butter; one of the captain's sons, James, was gored to death by a bull. Family albums might contain photographs of tennis at Windermere, of debonair George Draper flying in for a visit and flipping his biplane on the hydro lines above a recently plowed field, but this was a hardworking, highly individualistic, close-knit clan, "stoutly cl[inging] to British traditions." Of course they weren't the Whiteoaks, but it is certainly no accident that when Mazo moved into Trail Cottage, centenarian Adeline, royalist Renny, English-educated uncles, titled aunt, Canadian farmer Piers, and artist figures Eden and Finch all but commandeered her pencil.

As Dorothy Livesay has suggested, those critics who contended that the Whiteoaks weren't Canadian obviously never visited Clarkson when Mazo and Caroline lived there. It is somewhat ironic, though touching, that in her last talk with Mazo, Livesay, the author of "Day and Night" and other politically militant verse, should have joined her old neighbour in lamenting "the old days in Ontario when people did live as English landed gentry" ("Making of Jalna").

Jalna and Benares

Just as the Whiteoaks, though no doubt suggested to Mazo by family, friends, neighbours, and even strangers, were the product of her own imagination, Jalna, though inspired by several houses of her experience, was a fictional place. This having been said, I believe (despite Timothy Findley's contention that the Harrises of Clarkson are a red herring) that the central influence on Jalna's creation was Benares. This is not to deny the significance of the other large houses that played a part in the life of Mazo de la Roche prior to the publication of *Jalna*. The venerated home of the Whiteoaks was clearly a composite of several Southern Ontarian settings, boiled in the cauldron of Mazo's very active imagination.

One of the earliest architectural influences on Jalna must have been a romantic Gothic Revival house at Toronto's Jarvis and Wellesley Streets; some will remember it as Julie's Restaurant. Mazo's father moved his family to Cawthra Square, just off Jarvis Street, in 1900, and a year later Mazo lived at 469 Jarvis Street while studying at the Ontario School of Art. The Gothic Revival mansion at 515 Jarvis, built in 1868, was the home of Mrs. Massey Treble, whose father, Mr. Hart Massey, had purchased it in 1882. It was the sort of house that would appeal to Mazo's fancy, with turrets and battlements and a Moorish interior echoing that of Toronto's Massey Hall.

Mazo had come into the orbit of the Masseys through her family's friendship with the James Warnocks of Galt, Ontario, the town where Mazo and her parents had lived in the early 1890s. Like the Masseys, the Warnocks were part of the province's industrial plutocracy. When Hart Massey's grandsons Raymond (of acting fame) and Vincent (the future governor-general of Canada) were orphaned, Mrs. Warnock took the boys into her own household. One of the Warnock children, Amelia Beers, cousin to the Masseys, was to become one of Mazo's closest — and lifelong — friends, and would write under the pseudonym of Katherine Hale; her sister Anne's husband, Edward Dimock, became Mazo's stockbroker. Maisie Roche of Newmarket likely regarded the Masseys as colonial aristocracy; Mazo de la Roche, famous author, socialized with Raymond in England (where he suggested she adapt *Jalna* to the stage), and expressed horror at Vincent's appointment as the first Canadian-born governor-general.

Another likely influence on Jalna was Beverley, the Beardmore house in Acton. Today its once-splendid garden, which had resembled the large grounds of the fairy-tale Massey house in Toronto, is the site of two apartment buildings, products of the sort of "progress" that was anathema to Mazo. At the time the Roches lived on Acton's Main Street, however, Beverley was in its prime. The archives in the Fisher Rare Book Library contain a letter written to Ronald Hambleton by Miss Jean MacKenzie, whose father had been manager of the Dominion Inn, rival of W.R. Roche's Acton House. In it, Miss MacKenzie, surmising that the Beardmores and Roches would have had social relations through the Anglican Church, recalls that when her mother first read *Jalna*, the Whiteoaks immediately suggested the Beardmores to her.

Two other large Ontario houses embodying British traditions are located in a far more idyllic spot: Jackson's Point on Lake Simcoe. The first of these, Eildon Hall, was home to Mrs. Susan Sibbald, who came to Canada from Scotland in 1835 to determine whether her sons were living wicked lives in the colonies. She fell in love with Sutton Lodge and purchased it and its five-hundred-acre farm. (Jalna, though originally one thousand acres, is reduced to five hundred acres, thanks to the second-generation uncles' improvidence.) Mrs. Sibbald returned to Scotland the next year, after having arranged for the building of a church (shades of the Whiteoaks here, as well), but upon finding that her husband had died in her absence, she again crossed the Atlantic, family treasures in tow. This time, she transformed her farm into a magnificent estate, Eildon Hall, described by her son John as "the largest and most aristocratic looking place in this part of the country" (Beaton). Here, Old World manners were cultivated: "The Sibbalds had a full stable of horses and exotic gardens. While farm chores consumed a large part of the working day, the family still found it possible to continue certain customs associated with the gracious life they had led in Scotland" (Byers et al.). Substitute Ireland and England for Scotland, and you have a description of the life led by Captain Philip Whiteoak and his wife, Adeline, at Jalna.

Close to Eildon Hall is another stately home, The Briars, a

FIGURE 6

An old photograph of Beverley, the Beardmore house in Acton, now demolished.

Regency-style manor, built in 1839, that was purchased as a gentleman's residence in the 1870s by Mrs. Sibbald's eighth son, Frank. He added wings, a coach house, and an octagonal peacock house. Mazo and Caroline spent their last five summers at The Briars, which was by then a resort run by the Sibbald family; they stayed in lakeside cottage number 2. Mazo had vacationed at Lake Simcoe before, when she was a child. It was here that she had received word that one of her stories was to be published; it was one of her first acceptances. The repeated references to the area in *Ringing the Changes* testify to its importance in her life. And it was here that she was buried, in the cemetery of St. George's Church on Sibbald's Point, built in memory of Susan Sibbald.

All this evidence lends support to Timothy Findley's argument that Jalna is closely linked to The Briars; the Sibbalds, a matriarchal clan, he sees as the very model of the Whiteoaks. Yet when, in a radio interview Caroline Clement was asked about the origins of Jalna, she responded:

> [S]omeone's got the idea that it's the old Sibbald family of Sutton.... [W]ell old Mrs. Sibbald was a character and they were a family who settled here in very much the same style that the Whiteoaks did, as country gentry. But as a matter of fact, Miss de la Roche had never heard of the Sibbalds except she might have heard their name, but that was all when she wrote *Jalna*; it was compounded ... the background was very much compounded of her own family's background.

Of course, we would probably be wise to maintain a healthy scepticism when it comes to Caroline's disclaimers. She also insisted that the Whiteoaks weren't the Harrises and that Jalna wasn't Benares — "they like to think it is, but it really isn't" — but there is certainly no house, its history included, that Jalna resembles so closely as Benares.

I have already noted that in her autobiography Mazo wrote of *Jalna* as having been inspired by the traditions of the Clarkson area. Like Captain James Beveridge Harris of Benares, Captain Philip Whiteoak was drawn to the community because it was inhabited by retired British military and naval officers devoted to English values. Captain Harris, who belonged to Britain's Twenty-Fourth

FIGURE 7

Benares in the 1960s: "The old red house, behind the shelter of spruce and balsam, drew into itself as the winter settled in" (*Jalna*).

Regiment, purchased Benares in 1836, sold his commission, and moved to the 285-acre estate with his Irish wife and two children. Named after an Anglo-Indian military station, Benares was twice destroyed by fire, and was rebuilt in dusty-rose brick in 1857.

Readers of the Jalna chronicles will recall that Mazo's fictional house was built in 1854 by Captain Philip Whiteoak of the Hussars, who sold *his* commission to purchase the thousand-acre property. He and his Irish bride, Adeline, had fallen in love in an Indian garrison town, after which they named *their* Canadian homestead. It, too, is of rosy brick, its architectural features similar to, if grander than, those of Benares.

Both houses have stone foundations, deep basements where their kitchens are located, outdoor bake ovens, large drawing rooms, a ground-floor bedroom, frame outbuildings, a revered ancestral portrait of a handsome military officer — the list goes on. The first time I visited Benares I could almost hear old Adeline's parrot, Boney, croaking obscenities behind the shutters, almost glimpse red-haired Renny and blue-eyed Piers crossing the lawn on their way to the stable. Of course, the two houses have their differences — Jalna has three storeys to Benares' two (in order to accommodate all its visitors); French windows rather than six-pane sashes; five rather than four chimneys; walls and veranda adorned with Virginia creeper instead of the climbing roses that once graced Benares — but in their histories and appearance they bear an undeniable resemblance to one another.

In a letter written to her publisher, Alfred McIntyre, in 1927, de la Roche admitted that there was an old house, also built by a retired British officer, that "partially suggested" Jalna; she even advised him in another letter that she planned on taking a photograph of Benares to use on *Jalna*'s cover. And when the CBC television series of the early 1970s was in preproduction, shooting was slated to be done at Benares, though the location was shifted to a similar old house in Whitby when Mr. and Mrs. Geoffrey Sayers, who then occupied the ancestral home, learned that the period of filming was to be extended. Incidently, in 1993, Mr. Sayers advised the council of the city of Mississauga, into which Clarkson had been absorbed in the late 1960s, that Benares was indeed the property portrayed in the Jalna novels, and remarked that certain characters in the books possessed similarities to members of his family; earlier, in 1972, he told reporter Bernadette Andrews of the *Toronto Star*, "the Whiteoak family was hung loosely on my ancestors."

When, then, both Mazo and Caroline later argued that no one house was Jalna, they likely had complex motives. The most obvious of these is their firm belief that it is important to distinguish between fact and fiction. Yet while Caroline suggested that members of the Harris clan liked to think Benares was Jalna, their descendents, the Sayers, tell quite a different story — that the family was sick and tired of their privacy being invaded by, for example, carloads of middle-aged men who would arrive in Clarkson chanting "Jalna! Jalna!" Kathleen Sayers, Geoffrey's wife, bluntly stated the family's position in a letter to Ronald Hambleton: "She used our family home and background for her book — and for years we have wished she selected some other residence on which to base it. It has been a damned nuisance." Still, the three Sayers offspring who bequeathed Benares to the Ontario Heritage Foundation have emphasized the de la Roche connection to ensure the survival of the house.

Perhaps the most revealing comments on the relation between the two houses and their occupants came from Naomi Harris, Captain James Beveridge Harris's granddaughter. In 1967, the year before Miss Harris's death, Kathleen Sayers, in a second letter to Hambleton, observed of her husband's aunt, "She . . . takes a dim view of the Whiteoaks as a clan — 'such disreputable people!' — and strongly resents the general impression that they are based on HER family." Yet when asked by a reporter for the Toronto *Telegram* at the time of Mazo's death if Benares were really Jalna, Naomi Harris replied, "No. It's Benares, named after the place in India. I don't know why she had to change the name" ("Was Toronto Home 'Jalna'?").

Transcript: Barbara Larson

The setting: a log house — not a settlers' log house of the nineteenth century, but a commodious, elegantly furnished dwelling of the early 1920s, built by Beverley Sayers, husband to Annie Louise

Harris. Opposite me is the youngest of their three offspring, Barbara, born in 1920. She has just set before us a sachet from the late 1930s bearing a card that reads, "From the lavender walk at Vale House to the family of Log Bungalow." It is a gift from Mazo and Caroline. The scent of the lavender still lingers. Old books, family portraits, and heirlooms add to the atmosphere, which is that of an inhabited museum. The table is piled with scrapbooks and photo albums, from which Mrs. Barbara Larson produces — as though by legerdemain — Christmas cards from Mazo, snapshots of René and Esmée in England, carefully preserved letters on blue stationery from Caroline to Barbara's mother:

3 Ava Cres
Saturday
31 March 1966

My dear Ann[e],
It was nice to have your note and thank you for suggesting a call when I come your way. But, my dear, I never do! I want to keep the memory of that dear place undisturbed — to remember it as it was when Mazo and I were so happy in our ridiculous little cottage with its beautiful silver birches and pines, trailing arbutus and other wild flowers. So do come and see me some day.

I think you are very wise not to attempt driving in Toronto. The traffic is abominable and many of the drivers would seem to be trying to do someone a mischief — they are so careless of others.

What a long winter it has been. . . . I have always been accustomed to frequent changes and am missing it sadly.

I shall always think, with great affection, of your family and that dear spot as I knew it.

Love,
Caroline

3 Ava Cres
Wednesday [n.d.]

My dear Ann,
It is indeed sad that we no longer see anything of each other — and amazing that the years, so many of them, have

passed. . . . Now, but for some dear friends, I am much alone. So, you see, it is your duty to *come and* see me! . . .

Caroline

We travel through time in the opening and closing of envelopes, the exchange of sepia-tinted photographs and shadowy daguerreotypes.

Before me is a picture of Barbara Sayers when she was about seven years old. It was taken at Trail Cottage on one of her visits to Mazo and Caroline, who mailed it to her from Toronto around the time that *Jalna* won the *Atlantic Monthly* prize. And here are two other children, Esmée and René de la Roche — three years and eighteen months, respectively. The boy perches on the arm of his traditional-looking English nurse. A smiling, bundled-up Esmée holds the nurse's other hand. They are posed in the garden of the Rectory, Hawkchurch, in January 1932. "Do you mind if I tape this?" The spell is broken.

[I begin the interview.] Now, I understand that Trail Cottage stood on part of the original Benares estate, and that your mother had received a portion of this land as a wedding present.

[Barbara Larson begins to talk, and gradually the spell is recast . . .] *From my grandfather* [Arthur Harris]. *I don't remember whether it was a wedding present or after they were married. It was over a hundred acres . . . I have a feeling it was about one hundred and twenty-five acres.*

And Trail Cottage was part of what was called the Birchwood Subdivision?

Yes, it was, because my father, about 1922, sold a lot from the Birchwood Subdivision to Mazo. The Livesays had been already established there, nearby, and they knew Mazo. This is how she became aware of the subdivision.

What do you remember of Trail Cottage?

It was one room and dark and I always thought of it as very cosy. It had a screen door, and I had to be careful to hold it open to get the dog out. That was my favourite thing, to go over and walk Bunty.

You walked *Bunty?!*

Oh yes, I used to go <u>mainly</u> to visit her and see how they were, and I never stayed long. "Oh," they'd say, "Oh yes, here's Bunty."

Was Bunty blind then?

<u>Getting</u> blind, but I used to just take her for a walk, and then take her back. I never stayed long because Mazo was busy, always writing, and you knew that they didn't want children bothering them for any length of time. That was when I was six or seven. That picture I showed you was taken about that time: 1927. It would have been around the time of Jalna.

How would you describe Mazo's appearance as you remember her?

I always thought of her as being very sharp-faced — you know, sharp features — and very slight, with a sallow complexion. I felt that she was not very strong or healthy. She always struck me as being rather frail. And I suppose Caroline did, too, to a degree, mainly because she sort of <u>fluttered</u>. And she fluttered her eyelashes at you when she was talking to you — it may have had a lot to do with the fact that she even then was having trouble with her eyesight, but as she talked she blinked her eyes a lot. But Mazo was, as I say, frail.

Would you describe Caroline as more outgoing?

Yes, Caroline was warmer. They were both very kind to me and I loved them very much, but I always was more drawn to Caroline than I was to Mazo because Caroline was the one who put her arm about you, made you feel as though you were . . . wanted. She took more time with you. Mazo was very busy <u>thinking</u>, doing her own thing.

Do you remember the reaction of the community to Mazo's winning the prize for *Jalna*?

I remember people saying "Oh, isn't it nice?" and "Haven't you heard?" And if you ran into somebody . . . I suppose a lot of people talked about it. It was announced in the papers and it was announced on the radio, and that's early radio.

I remember Dorothy Livesay writing about how happy everyone was because Mazo and Caroline had never had a lot of money and . . .

No, and they hadn't! I mean they were struggling. Look at the way their cottage was furnished, or not furnished. There were large orange crates used for a lot of things (Mazo even used them for writing by the side of the road), and I remember cots — they were like canvas cots that they slept on.

Do you remember Fiddler's Hut, which Mazo refers to in the Jalna novels?

I know mother remembered Fiddler's Hut. Jock, the fiddler?

That's right. His story's told in *Jalna* — how Fiddler Jock used to play at weddings and parties but overindulged one night and, unable to find his way home, ended up frozen in a haystack. Dorothy Livesay wrote about him — she claimed the hut was on their property, at Woodlot.

It was closer to Benares, on my grandfather's property. Mother had this picture of Jock's cottage. I'm sad to say that it disappeared at the time my aunt died and my brother and his wife took over Benares.

Would it have been standing when Mazo was here?

In the early 1920s part of it might have been . . .

What about the Miss Laceys in *Jalna*? Their father was an admiral and had a place called The Moorings.

Well, I'll bet anything Mazo had Captain Skynner's place down on the lake in mind, because that was called The Anchorage.

The Anchorage! Oh, that's wonderful! Captain Skynner . . .

Well, the captain's house is now part of the Bradley Museum [in Clarkson] — it's one of the buildings. They pulled it up from the lakeshore because it used to be down where the cement plant has taken over. The Bradley house and all those houses along the lakeshore were some of the first settlements in the area. The old Anchorage was a house that my mother recalled the captain had put on a barge and brought over from Toronto. I remember it as a kid — I've got pictures of it — and then when they wanted to make it part of the museum they brought it up to the Bradley house. I used to go down there for picnics when I was a child, when the Hannings lived there. Captain Skynner lived

FIGURE 8

Captain Skynner's The Anchorage, an 1830s Regency cottage in Clarkson.

FIGURE 9

René and Esmée, possibly at Benares, in the early 1930s.
From the Harris scrapbooks.

there originally. Skynner's granddaughter, Emily, married my great-uncle William Henry Draper, the chief justice's son.

Yes, Piers and Pheasant move into The Moorings in *The Master of Jalna*, after he and Renny have a quarrel.

I'll bet that's what it was. [Laughter.] I mean the captain and The Anchorage, and the admiral and The Moorings — that's pretty close, isn't it?

Do you remember Mazo and Caroline coming back after their first trip to Europe?

Well, I remember them coming over with Esmée and René. And that would have been in the thirties. I don't know how many times they went over. I think they were here probably about 1932 to 1933, because that's when I remember going down to the lake with the kids — I took them down with their nanny . . . but I went down and played with them and I helped look after them. (I liked little kids.) Esmée was . . . I kept on thinking of her as being like Alice in Wonderland with this beautiful English accent and this long, long, shining, beautiful hair — blond. She was a very dainty little girl and René was a very cute little boy — a stocky little boy. But that would have been, I think, 1932.

Do you remember the circumstances surrounding Trail Cottage's demolition?

It happened when the subdivision was completed by my brother after the war. The lots had always been on a plan that my father had drawn up back in the twenties, but it had never become a fact or roads put through until after the war, and then suddenly my mother found that she was being charged garbage collection and taxes on every lot that wasn't even developed.

How do the Magraths fit into your family?

My Grandmother Harris was a Magrath. Her grandfather was the first rector of the Anglican Church in Erindale [St. Peter's].

The one place Caroline would acknowledge Mazo to have directly used in the Jalna novels.

I do know that Caroline and Mazo recognized that there was a problem.

Because they knew that the family was still living in the house. I think they backtracked when they realized that all that publicity was causing problems for our family. Mazo had said to her publisher that she wanted to get a picture of Benares — that was when she first published Jalna; *and actually, when the* Whiteoaks *play came to North America she sent the set designer out. Yes. It's definite; as far as I'm concerned it couldn't be more definite than it is — I think that all, or any, of the denials are simply because they did know that it caused all kinds of consternation and problems for my aunt and grandparents when people insisted upon tramping up to the house with their cameras . . . and through the gardens. They didn't care where they went, and peered through the windows and made life uncomfortable. And this is why my aunt became so antagonistic: she just got fed up with these people coming, and so she denied anything about it. She never read the books — she'd heard enough about them.*

But you had. When did you read the books?

I read Jalna *originally when I was a teenager, and I've read bits and pieces of them. But now I'm going to have to do it: I've too many people asking me about the stories and the people in them, so I'd better smarten up and read them.*

People didn't have this obsession with publicity then.

It never occurred to us that just because somebody wrote something about a house that we lived in that this was a publicity thing or that you might become famous! Somebody had just written about the area and it happened to be my grandparents' home and I never thought anything about it. It never — not even once — occurred to me that there was anything significant about it.

Jalna

Ringing the Changes documents *Jalna*'s winning the ten-thousand-dollar *Atlantic Monthly* open competition for "most interesting novel" in early 1927. Upon completion of the manuscript, Mazo submitted it to the Macmillan Company of New York, with which she was already under contract, for consideration. She then learned of the *Atlantic Monthly* contest and, thinking there was only a slim chance of her receiving the prize, sent off a carbon copy of her typescript. Concluding, after several weeks, that "This sort of double life could not go on," Mazo, imagination inflamed, even considered the possibility that she "might end in prison!" She contacted the editors of the *Atlantic*, only to be told that her entry was one of three — out of over one-thousand submissions — that had been short-listed.

Once she had been assured by Macmillan that she would be released from her contract should *Jalna* be selected by the *Atlantic* and Little, Brown, the company that was to publish the winning novel after its serialization in the magazine, Mazo slipped into one of her periods of extreme anxiety, and Caroline lamented that she had entered the competition in the first place. When Mazo received confirmation from Ellery Sedgwick, editor of the *Atlantic*, that *Jalna* had won, the "cruel suspense of that waiting" gave way to fears about the "ordeal of publicity," and Mazo, Caroline, and Bunty fled from Toronto to a guest house in Niagara Falls. There Mazo developed a bad cold and cough. When the biographical questionnaire from Little, Brown arrived, Caroline filled it in because Mazo was too ill to respond.

Finch Whiteoak's response to inheriting his grandmother's legacy in *Whiteoaks of Jalna* clearly expresses the conflicting emotions that Mazo felt on the heels of her own stunning success. But before we look more closely at this novel, *Jalna*'s sequel, we must return to the quieter days at Trail Cottage, the period during which *Jalna* was written. In her autobiography, Mazo recalls that *Jalna* was originally conceived as a play about a brother and sister, who would emerge as Renny and Meg Whiteoak. Thus, when *Jalna* and *Whiteoaks of Jalna* were combined into the play *Whiteoaks* in 1936, Mazo had, in terms of genre, come full circle. She did not, however, actually begin writing the novel until 1925, the time of its action. That summer, in the simple cottage in Clarkson, the Whiteoaks forced their way into their maker's consciousness: "From the very first the characters created themselves. They leaped from my imagination and from memories of my own family. The grandmother, Adeline Whiteoak,

FIGURE 10

An 1814 portrait of Major General John Harris (1760–1833), by Charles Allingham. Allingham exhibited at the Royal Academy and Dublin Gallery. The major was the father of James Beveridge Harris, Benares's patriarch.

refused to remain a minor character but arrogantly, supported on either side by a son, marched to the centre of the stage." Gran stepped forth from Mazo's memories of her paternal grandmother, Sarah Bryan Roche, and, more directly, from her memories of her great-grandmother, Sarah Danford Bryan. Great-grandmother Bryan's portrait is described in *Ringing the Changes*, her youthful features suggesting those of the young Mrs. Philip Whiteoak who, along with the captain, had sat for a fashionable artist in London before coming to Canada. This painting of Mazo's revered ancestor complements the portrait of Major General John Harris that has presided over Benares since 1837. The portraits of Philip and Adeline Whiteoak, the founders of Jalna, are family icons whose power is not completely revealed until the last novel in the chronology, *Centenary at Jalna*.

Most notably, Renny Whiteoak, Philip and Adeline's eldest grandson, displays certain of W.R. Roche's attributes. Renny and Mazo's father share not only an overt and overpowering masculinity, but also a love of pedigreed dogs and horses and an indifference to automobiles; a devil-may-care attitude towards practical matters countered by a passionate love of life; and, not least, adoration for an only daughter, a devotion that binds Freudian papa to worshipping tomboy. But Renny's only daughter was to come later, born in *The Master of Jalna*, and, in spite of the close bond between Renny and young Adeline, Mazo did not, by her own admission, feel completely at one with Renny's daughter or, for that matter, any of her female characters. In *Jalna*, and even more so in *Whiteoaks of Jalna*, it was Finch, Renny's half-brother, with whom Mazo most completely identified.

Finch's status as autobiographical persona is already conspicuous in *Jalna*. Finch is not only an artist figure, but also an outsider. Although his attempted suicide and emotional breakdowns occur in the next two Whiteoaks novels, in *Jalna* Finch suffers from an overactive imagination, sexual anxieties, morbid religious fantasies, self-doubt, frustrated artistic genius, and a desperate longing for freedom. Awkward and angular, he stews in his own juices, marginalized within his own family.

To Finch's humiliations at the hands of his virile brothers Piers and Renny, Mazo adds the insults levelled by the manly Whiteoaks against the women who marry into their generation. When Pheasant, Piers's wife, observes that she and Alayne, brother Eden's bride, have not had the opportunity to bathe in the lake at a family picnic, Renny tells her that it's "too cold for girls." Pheasant points out to Renny that her sex is, in fact, better able to endure the cold, and remarks that while the Whiteoak males work and play, the women are expected to twiddle their thumbs.

Around the time *Jalna* won the *Atlantic Monthly* prize, Gertrude Pringle, Mazo's landlady at 86 Yorkville Avenue in Toronto, wrote two articles in which she noted Mazo's "masculine Spanish name" and described her nearly fifty-year-old tenant as having "something of a gallant boy in her bearing," "an almost boyish air." Caroline she referred to as Mazo's "chum." Dorothy Livesay, in a reminiscence of Mazo's days at Trail Cottage, remembered her neighbour's "gaunt, thin, rather neuter frame," and observed that, upon her return from Europe in the 1930s, Mazo "strode in, more masculine and assured than I had remembered her, her wit crackling, her musical laugh ringing" ("Making of Jalna"). Mazo could not, apparently, escape such comparisons, and even in these commentaries there is an inherent devaluing of the feminine (or "neuter"!) and a privileging of the masculine. No wonder Finch, nursing his fragile sexual identity, ends up sequestered in a cove, begging to be left alone!

Although Pheasant, Alayne, Finch, and Eden offer a critique of Whiteoak masculinity, Mazo's own allegiances are complex. Piers's sadistic treatment of Finch throughout the novel does not diminish his younger brother's hero worship; indeed, it seems to contribute to it. And, although those outside the family resist it, Renny's patriarchal nature is presented as having an elemental appeal. It is true that Alayne, before succumbing to the animal magnetism of her brother-in-law, thinks of Renny as having an "inflated opinion of his own importance as head of the house," and that Meg even moves out of Jalna when she comes up against her brother's masculine authority; but whether in church or at home, Renny is chieftain of the tribe.

Whatever our feelings towards Renny might be, it is well-nigh impossible to resist the most important character in the novel: Jalna itself. The old house has an atmosphere that affects all who enter its

FIGURE 11

St. Peter's Anglican Church (built in 1887) today. The church's first rector was Reverend James Magrath, whose granddaughter Mary married Arthur Harris, son of James Beveridge Harris.

doors — characters and readers alike. This power was well understood by the creators of *Jalna*, the French television series, in which the sprawling chateau in the forest is the real hero. Jalna has a soul; indeed, Mazo placed this soul in the basement kitchen, whose low ceiling, brick floor, and stone fireplace have absorbed "memories of the past, long-gone Christmas dinners, christening feasts, endless roasts and boilings" (*Jalna*). The old house also absorbs the passions of its occupants, and they, in turn, are infused by its psychic energy. At night, Jalna settles down by hunching itself against the darkness; in winter, like those under its protection, it draws inward, cutting itself off from the rest of the world. Among the scenes that linger longest in the reader's memory are those in which various Whiteoaks stand before Jalna's mellow brick walls and silently commune in a fellowship of love.

When Alayne Archer first views Jalna on a perfect autumn day, it is draped in Virginia creeper, bathed in golden sunlight, surrounded by lawns and orchards. Although Jalna has "the appearance of an old manorial farmhouse" (*Jalna*), it is ineradicably stamped with its own personality, not, as Northrop Frye and others have suggested, a pseudo-English house, but a farm in the southern Ontario countryside. What is remarkable here is Mazo's fusion of setting and characters. The life force courses through both. And if the old house is an actor, so, too, is nature, possessing its own smooth-sounding, mysterious language, the language spoken and understood by the Whiteoaks.

Beyond Jalna's woodlands, stream, and fields towers the church. Like St. Peter's of Erindale, its prototype, the Evandale sanctuary is perched high on a wooded knoll. Built in the 1850s by Captain Philip Whiteoak, it is the scene of those memorable Sunday-morning pilgrimages made by Gran Whiteoak in her old phaeton pulled by two immaculately groomed bay mares. They wind their way up the narrow road to the sound of honking horns and mumbled curses.

Still impressive in spite of the encroaching Mississauga traffic, St. Peter's is home to a churchyard exactly like that described in *Jalna*, except that "Magrath" rather than "Whiteoak" is carved on the granite plinth that rises from the family plot, enclosed by an iron fence. Here, on a dark evening, one might well expect to glimpse a distraught Finch kneeling on the mounds of the dead. Mazo's critics have chided her for repeating details such as those of the family plot — its low fence festooned with iron chains from which dangle little spiked balls — in one novel after another, but to her readers they must have functioned as signposts. Mazo was, after all, more of a storyteller than an artificer.

We receive a similar feeling of comfort in *Jalna* when we hear of Mistwell, Brancepeth, and Stead, where Piers and Pheasant, the illegitimate child of neighbour Maurice Vaughan, are secretly married. Readers of *Possession* might very well raise an eyebrow when in *Jalna*, Renny has horse dealings with Hobbs from "up Mistwell way," for here is the very man whom Derek Vale first encountered on the road to Grimstone. In *Whiteoaks of Jalna*, Mazo goes one step further, including Mr. Vale of Mistwell himself in a duck-shooting party! Whiteoak country has, with some justification, been compared to Faulkner's Yoknapatawpha County.

Mazo might also be likened to Faulkner on the basis of her political conservatism, which is already evident in the pristine air of *Jalna*. The pastoral ideal of the Big House as the soul of the family goes hand-in-glove with the Loyalist myth. When, for example, Piers, harangued about his elopement, threatens to leave Jalna for the United States, the Whiteoaks react with predictable horror: Gran exclaims that it would kill her. Renny quickly takes command: this is his family, his tribe. Piers will remain in the ancestral home. End of discussion.

Yet those who are listening will hear the first whisperings of the winds of change, which eventually reach gale force, early in the novel when the narrator informs us that, shortly after Jalna's completion in the 1850s, Captain and Mrs. Philip Whiteoak already "felt themselves cut off from the mother country, though they sent their children to England to be educated." Now, sixty years later, the Whiteoak offspring study at home, and Adeline grieves for a time when the wood pigeons were so plentiful that their flocks cast a great shadow. But while this gloom deepens over the next thirty years, in *Jalna* the tone is primarily celebratory, and what is being feted is life itself.

Like *Possession* and *Delight*, *Jalna* places much emphasis on the instinctive life, on spontaneity, joy, and freedom. Tradition is extremely important, but not (yet) oppressive. As do those she uses in her two previously published novels, the tropes Mazo employs in *Jalna* express an overriding pagan joy in the natural world. Characters are likened to animals, flowers, and trees, and those who are awarded the most figures of speech are most in tune with nature. These tropes thus link the Whiteoaks to the pastoral myth. Of course, a myth is exactly that — coming from the Greek *mythos*, a legend — and in creating the Whiteoaks Mazo was not only heavily drawing on local and family history but also actively engaged in mythmaking, in freely blending realism and romance. Yet, from the beginning of the Jalna series it seems inevitable that Mazo's pastoral ideal will crumble under the weight of history and time, that the Play will be invaded by a reality far nastier than Mrs. Handsomebody.

Whiteoaks of Jalna

I never lived at all
Until the thrill of the moment when
My heart stood still.
           — Rodgers and Hart, "My Heart Stood Still"

It is the spring of 1928. This popular tune from Richard Rodgers and Lorenz Hart's *A Connecticut Yankee* fills the air at a late-night dance in Toronto. The orchestra — not unlike an orchestra to which Mazo and Caroline belonged when, at the beginning of the century, they lived on Jarvis Street — consists of first and second mandolins, a flute, a banjo (Caroline's instrument), and a piano (Mazo's). Finch Whiteoak, unbeknownst to his family, is at the keyboard, having what he will later realize is the best time of his life. The orchestra's repertory is extremely limited, so again and again its members perform the same song, finally erupting into the lyrics as the hour passes four. Afterwards, having once more played Rodgers's melody in a dingy restaurant where the musicians have been plied with liquor, Finch and George Fennel, the banjo-playing son of

Evandale's rector, boisterously stagger about the city streets, arriving home after sunrise.

At Jalna, the besotted Finch is first surveyed by Rags, the Whiteoaks' supercilious servant, and then set upon by Renny and Piers. The result is a particularly nasty scene: the discovery of Finch's drunkenness leads to the disclosure of his involvement with the orchestra. Even more humiliating, however, is Piers's reading of a note accidentally dropped on the floor by his younger brother, a letter from Finch's effete and sexually ambiguous friend Arthur Leigh, a wealthy city boy. Addressing him as "Dearest" and "Darling" Finch, Arthur complains to his friend that the "clarity of their relationship" has been "clouded." Piers and Renny give vent to their rage and disgust, calling the affair "neurotic" and Leigh a "rotter." Finch breaks into tears. He's on his way to the nervous breakdown and attempted suicide that follow his psychological abuse by the family when Gran Whiteoak wills him her fortune.

On the surface, Mazo's life after the success of *Jalna* may not appear to have much in common, save for piano playing, with that of eighteen-year-old Finch. When *Whiteoaks of Jalna* was published, in 1929, Mazo was fifty and a celebrated literary success. Yet she had just recovered from the second nervous breakdown of her life, which she had suffered during the writing of this most personal of her Whiteoak narratives. "I was one with Finch," she wrote, "for he and I had much in common. I was (at times) one with Renny, for he and I had much in common. At other times I was against him" (*Ringing*). She is most clearly against the patriarch of Jalna for posing a threat to Finch's artistic spirit, to his sexual identity, to the very wellspring of his selfhood and personal freedom.

Mazo suffered her first breakdown when she was only slightly older than Finch, and he brings to the novel many of the attributes of her nature that are consciously and unconsciously expressed in *Ringing the Changes*. For example, although it is his younger brother, Wakefield, who will come under the influence of Roman Catholicism, Finch is haunted by religious doubts and anxieties, often manifested in hallucinatory visions. As we have seen, Mazo's breakdown followed her viewing of *Everyman* and subsequent kneeling at the Stations of the Cross, in direct defiance of her family.

Finch is painfully uncomfortable with his sexual identity — called a sissy by Renny, accused of homosexuality by Piers, confused by his feelings towards Arthur Leigh and Arthur's sister, Ada. In her autobiography, Mazo confesses her aversion to being touched by males, comparing herself to a "highly strung filly that will not endure a hand laid on her"; erupts in jealousy when the boy next door holds and caresses Caroline's "thin little hand"; tells her readers how she enjoyed attracting men, but would then fiercely withdraw, looking on "sex as rather silly."

Most notably, Finch is frustrated in his attempts to become an artist: Renny criticizes him for acting at the university, cuts off his music lessons as punishment for academic failure, and later prohibits him from playing with the orchestra. Mazo, though encouraged by her parents and Caroline in her artistic endeavours, suggests to us that there was a less supportive attitude within the larger households where she spent her formative years. Grandpa Lundy's "icy silence" abruptly quells the girls' "ridiculous games" in Parkdale; the Lundys deplore "extravagance and [take] no pains to hide their disapproval" of those who "crav[e] beauty to surround them." When Mazo's father reads her first published story to her Grandmother Roche, she is patently bored by it, longing for her lunch. Mazo slinks from the room during the reading, but afterwards finds her grandmother gratefully approaching the lunch table as the dog drags the magazine containing the story under the sofa.

Finch, lying in bed, feeling that his head has become solid inside while sharp pains attack its surface, finds himself "an outcast in his own home, unspeakably alone" (*Whiteoaks of Jalna*). Haunted by his ongoing crisis of identity, he studies his hand, seeing it as a tool for making art, a symbol of potential creativity. Mazo, unable to leave her bed because of vertigo, violent headaches, and, later, hallucinations, feels herself an alien in the presence of her own family. Her hand and arm become paralysed — she cannot even move a pencil. A year passes before she can write a letter, two more before she recovers (though she claims that her physical strength never did return fully).

Finally achieving unity with the cosmos through the therapeutic influence of music, Finch breaks with the Whiteoaks by running away to New York City, though he is secretly relieved when Uncle Ernest arrives to fetch him home to the protective enclave of Jalna.

Mazo, in need of "a complete change of air and scene" (*Ringing*), journeys by herself to Georgian Bay, losing touch with her family. When she is finally reunited with Caroline, she throws herself into the Play with new vigour, her creative juices once again flowing, her hand moving.

And then there is the matter of Finch's inheritance. Surely this is where his story intersects not with Mazo's account of her first breakdown, but with her description of the moment when *her* heart stood still: the moment she learned she had won the *Atlantic Monthly* prize for *Jalna*. We might expect that this event would have heralded an end to the years of anxiety, of frequent moves, of restless striving. But this was not the case. I have already mentioned the nerve-racking effect that the suspense of being a finalist and the fear of having to cope with the publicity after her win had upon Mazo. In *Ringing the Changes*, she maintains that her initial fears quickly gave way to manic elation as reporters crowded into the living room on Yorkville Avenue, where Mazo basked in the limelight amidst telegrams, letters, and flowers. Favourable reviews appeared in the journals. *Jalna*'s author was toasted by the governor-general, received a letter from the prime minister, the Right Honourable Mackenzie King. Dinners were given by the nation's literary societies, and Mazo received a life-size drawing of Bunty from Toronto's Arts and Letters Club after Edward Weeks of the *Atlantic Monthly* addressed its members.

Whiteoaks of Jalna provides an analogue to what Mazo must have experienced in the face of all these public appearances, for, on the opening night of the play in which he is acting, Finch fluctuates between wanting to be swallowed by the earth and feeling he's walking on air. Once on stage, however, he becomes the star of the evening; and everyone to whom I have spoken who ever heard Mazo lecture confirms that even in her final years she was a commanding presence at the podium — charming, witty, and somewhat formidable. Still, all this role-playing must have taken a heavy toll on such a shy, ordinarily retiring individual; this conjecture is borne out by the events of the coming year. Sustaining Mazo and Caroline in "these pressing and almost breathless days" was the Play — the make-believe world "so much more satisfying than the material world" (*Ringing*). Then the spring weather made it possible for them to benefit from the tranquility of Trail Cottage. When summer arrived, however, Mazo and Caroline, remaining true to the bold pattern they had set for their life together, chose to head off to Rockport, Massachusetts. Here, in the attic of a house overlooking the harbour, Mazo worked on the opening chapters of the second of the Jalna novels.

Although Mazo suggests in *Ringing the Changes* that Bunty's death was largely responsible for the breakdown that she experienced while working on the *Whiteoaks of Jalna* the following winter, her collapse was clearly the result of many types of stress. Just before writing of Bunty's final days, she remarks that speech making and the "demands of society" interrupted her work. Ostensibly a reference to parties and late evenings, the phrase "demands of society" also implies her public's expectations when it came to her fulfilling certain roles. In her autobiography, Mazo also mourns the death, the previous spring, of the last of her father's family, her Uncle Francis (his name was Gallicized as François): he had suffered an "overpowering breakdown," allegedly brought about by a demanding wife. Both sides of Mazo's family had experienced similar neuroses. Her mother succumbed to long bouts of nervous exhaustion; Mazo earlier describes how the cords in Alberta Roche's neck stood out like the strings of an instrument on which a wild tune was being played, and how her eyes had "a look of strange intensity."

That winter, Mazo exhibited symptoms almost identical to those she assigned Finch, a pain creeping across her temples and then down the back of her head, lodging in her neck. As she had during her 1903 collapse, she found herself unable to write even so much as a postcard: "I lived and had my being in pain," she recalls in her autobiography, which begins to read like *The Bell Jar* as Mazo recounts "electrical treatments" whose only effect was to "dull [her] memory." She could no longer distinguish between the days; her life had become a continuum of pain and alienation from those around her. Fortunately, a nurse finally talked Mazo into discontinuing the shock treatments, and, under Caroline's care, she slowly fought her way back to mental and physical health. The two cousins returned to Trail Cottage, and Mazo moved towards the completion of what is arguably her finest novel. It was at this time that she became possessed by Finch.

In *Whiteoaks of Jalna*, Finch's inheritance, like Mazo's prize, proves a mixed blessing. Although Adeline Whiteoak's legacy promises him liberation when he comes of age in two years' time, its immediate effect is to pitch him into hysteria, culminating in his wish for death. (How appropriate that Mazo's persona should try to drown himself in the lake that symbolizes freedom throughout her writing!) Fuelling Finch's movement towards dissolution — he is appropriately rescued by his tubercular brother Eden, the other alienated artist in the clan, who has been booted out of Jalna for his sexual misconduct with Piers's wife — is the relentless harassment he receives from his family. To clan chieftain Renny, the "trouble" with his half-brothers is their attraction to poetry and music, a weakness inherited from their "flibbertigibbet" mother, Mary Wakefield. Finch recognizes that he and Eden are "travelers in a region which the rest of the family [does] not enter . . . palmers to the shrine of beauty"; but to his Uncle Nicholas he is simply "hag-ridden by art."

Paradoxically, the strength Finch begins to feel in the closing chapters of the novel — composed as Mazo's own vitality returned to her — comes from his memory of Gran Whiteoak, whose bequest has precipitated his near self-destruction. This legacy, like Mazo's windfall, brings on a life-threatening crisis, yet out of the ashes of his former self Finch arises. Having confessed to his centenarian grandmother his deep fear of life, Finch witnesses her courage in the face of death. Adeline Whiteoak's final words, in response to the suggestion that she's been beaten at backgammon, are, "Me beaten? Not a bit of it. I won't have it! I've won." As their eyes join in victory ("Gammon!"), Finch sees the old lady's spirit leave her body, as "staunch and stubborn" as ever.

Mazo's own brush with spiritual death led her to infuse the lives of this imaginary family, more real to her than life, with the sense of her own experience. Was it the courage of her own hearty matriarchs that helped Mazo recover her artistic strength? Was it Caroline's love? Or was it some secret evocation of her own private muse? *"This is what you have,"* whispers a disembodied voice (Findley, *Wars*). What we do know is that Mazo was now prepared to spread her wings — across the Atlantic. "Gammon!"

Finch's Fortune

The day before Mazo and Caroline departed from New York to sail to Europe, 9 January 1929, was frenetic. On board the *S.S. Vulcania*, about to make her maiden voyage, the *Atlantic Monthly* and Little, Brown cosponsored a luncheon in honour of *Jalna*'s author, attended by seventy members of the New York publishing world, including critics and the media. That evening, Mazo and Caroline attended an old melodrama revived by Christopher Morley (who had written the foreword to *Explorers of the Dawn*) at his theatre in Hoboken. They arrived back at the *Vulcania* and spirited themselves up the gangway just before the midnight sailing time. It was the end of a long day, and Mazo's elation had turned to exhaustion. As she lay on her berth, reflecting on the postluncheon photography session during which, festooned with violets, she had been surrounded on deck by sixteen men from the book trade, Mazo began to weep. "I thought I knew what movie stars felt when they took an overdose of sleeping tablets and ended all publicity," she recalled in *Ringing the Changes*.

In *Finch's Fortune*, Finch Whiteoak, now twenty-one and in possession of his grandmother's hundred-thousand-dollar legacy, decides to take his two elderly uncles to England. Before their departure, Finch falls prey to a number of anxieties, finally losing himself by playing the piano. Like Mazo and Caroline, Finch and Uncles Nicholas and Ernest choose New York, rather than Montreal, as their port; and once he boards the ship, which also leaves at midnight, Finch enters into an extremely self-referential relationship with his creator. The door to the stateroom next to his is open, and he sees that the floor is strewn with flower baskets and boxes filled with roses. In the passage stand two women reading one of the several telegrams that they clutch in their hands. Finch, who has hitherto been misreading the actions of virtually every member of his family, and who is oblivious to their efforts to manipulate him after he acquires his fortune, assumes from the telegrams that the two ladies have received bad news from home, yet the boxes of flowers suggest quite the opposite. Mazo employs a similar self-directed irony at the end of her next novel, *Lark Ascending*, when two women of nearly fifty come into contact with the heroine: at this time in her career she appeared to enjoy making such appearances in the manner of Alfred Hitchcock, her playfulness extending to the subtraction of a few years from the age of one of the women.

Although Mazo and Caroline first explored the Mediterranean, which provided material for short fiction and *Lark Ascending*, from the time they arrived in England, their itinerary bears a marked resemblance to that of the Whiteoaks. Finch and his septuagenarian uncles spend time in London before heading to Devon, where Lady Augusta Buckley, Finch's widowed aunt and their sister, has her country house. Mazo and Caroline also went to London before venturing on to Devon, and Mazo's description of her first impression of that city is mirrored in Finch's response.[3]

Mazo and Caroline arrived at the house they had rented, The Cottage, in Winkleigh, Devon, in late May. It was during the two months they spent there that they discovered Seckington, an old Winkleigh farmhouse. They leased it, but before moving in they rented a furnished house on the Cornish coast and then a rural cottage in Worcestershire. They followed this sojourn with a month at Oxford, and then, finally, returned to Seckington. Mazo imaginatively transformed the farmhouse into Lady Augusta's home, Lyming Hall, in the fictional village of Nymet Crews. Lest there be any question on this score, in *Ringing the Changes* she describes the appearance on Christmas Eve of the waits (or carolers) in the midst of a fierce gale that renders them inaudible; in *Finch's Fortune* the very same waits appear at Lyming Hall, where their voices are also torn away by gale-force winds. The same biographical-fictional nexus exists in Mazo's descriptions of a hunt.

Beyond these physical correspondences, *Finch's Fortune* is fascinating because so much of that which was central to Mazo's life is expressed through not only its protagonist and his circumstances, but also through other characters and the events that occur in their lives. Finch suffers what he describes as "a kind of nervous breakdown," during which he is assailed by severe headaches, and Alayne Archer, now married to Renny Whiteoak, also experiences an extreme pain in her head, pounding against the back of her neck exactly as Mazo's did. Earlier in the novel, George Fennel (who plays the banjo, like Caroline) describes to Finch his childhood fear of a big, white stuffed owl in a niche in the rectory's stairway; as I noted earlier, in *Ringing the Changes* Mazo recalls her terror of a great white owl perched halfway up her maternal grandfather's stairs. George uses the story to teach Finch a lesson about letting his imagination run wild; Mazo recalls how she became so involved in fancying the owl's activities that her "imagination [flew] away" with her, and tells us that Caroline only laughed at her cousin's attempts to scare her with owl stories.

At Lady Buckley's, Finch raids the bookcase in his aunt's dressing room, more "saturated with the personality of Augusta" than "any other room in the house." He finds Sir Walter Scott's *The Lady of the Lake* and Rhoda Broughton's *Cometh Up as a Flower*, as well as several romantic works by writers such as Baroness Orczy and Anthony Hope (Hawkins). In her autobiography, Mazo says that her happiest hours were spent reading with her parents, her father a fan of Sir Walter Scott, her mother of Rhoda Broughton; her favourite memories are of draping her "growing length" against her father's chest in his easy chair, the two engrossed in H. Rider Haggard.

Yet another example of Mazo's projecting herself into her novel's characters involves young Pauline Lebraux of Fox Farm, adjacent to Jalna. Pauline, a thin, long-limbed fifteen year old, remembers being read to by *her* now-deceased father:

> It had been ecstasy to her to lie in his arms, her cheek against the soft cloth of his coat, gazing up into his olive-skinned face, admiring the full curve of his lips beneath his little black moustache, the hairs of which were strong and glittering and were twisted at the ends into two little spikes, so sharp that they pricked you if a kiss was misdirected. Then, as she lay in his arms, they would whisper endearments and plan what they meant to do in the future. She would never leave him — never, never leave him.

Pauline's sexually sublimated relationship with her Freudian papa not only links her to *Possession*'s Grace Jerrold, but also anticipates the bond between young Adeline Whiteoak (her great-grandmother's namesake) and Adeline's father, Renny. An interesting gloss to this passage is that Tony Lebraux, Pauline's father, had pronounced Renny Whiteoak's name René, the name Mazo was to give to the boy she and Caroline adopted the year *Finch's Fortune* was published.

The most dramatic inscription of actuality into this narrative concerns not a person but a dog. In *Ringing the Changes*, Mazo tells the harrowing story — to which I have already alluded in my discussion of *Possession* — of how the family's Irish terrier, Barney, was savagely stabbed to death with pitchforks by the hired men at Rochedale when they thought the hysterical dog had rabies. This story is reproduced almost verbatim in *Finch's Fortune*: an Irish terrier given to Renny by Clara Lebraux, Pauline's mother, is overcome by the heat and stabbed to death by ignorant, pitchfork-wielding farm labourers at Jalna.

In both versions of the story the family patriarch is away in the city; in both the hysterical terrier has followed a horse onto the road in scorching heat; in both the hired men, in attempting to shoot the overwrought animal, are unable to discharge the master's gun; in both a youth from Glasgow brutally continues to pierce the dog's body after its death; in both the Irish terrier is named Barney. Renny is so furious with Alayne for having handed his gun to the men that he unfairly blames her for Barney's death, resulting in the two not speaking to one another for five days, and contributing to Alayne's decision to leave Jalna to visit a dying aunt. Even in *Return to Jalna*, which is set in the postwar period, Renny is still nursing the hurt he felt at his dog's murder. Interestingly, Mazo does not detail her father's reaction to similar news upon his return from Toronto, though it was a white-lipped Alberta Roche who handed her husband's gun to the farm manager. All these correspondences provide insight into the close relation between Mazo's life and her writing, yet it would be a great injustice to the powers of Mazo de la Roche's imagination to suggest that her writing was always directly based on the world of her immediate experience. Clearly, this exceptional incident had such an impact on her that she felt compelled to express it vividly in her fiction.

In contrast to this direct inscription of life into art is Mazo's discussion in her autobiography of the conception of certain characters. One such creation in *Finch's Fortune* is Sarah Court, a cousin of Finch's who, though in love with him, marries his best friend, Arthur Leigh. Mazo recalls,

> We had been sitting at lunch at our hotel in Oxford when two women entered the dining-room. One was old, one young. The younger so fascinated me that I could hardly keep my eyes off her. The convolutions of her black hair, the marble pallor of her skin, the strange, gliding rigidity of her walk, her secret smile. "Don't stare so," said Caroline, but how could I help staring? There glided, there smiled, there sat Sarah Court, one of the principal characters in my next novel.

From this simple germ — to use Henry James's term — Mazo would create a character who, after Arthur's drowning in *The Master of Jalna*, would go on to marry Finch in *Whiteoak Harvest*, bear him a child in *Wakefield's Course*, and die in an automobile accident in *Return to Jalna*, plaguing the Whiteoaks, particularly Finch, along the way.

Finch himself sprang from another brief encounter. The rumour mill has long attributed his creation to Mazo's friendship with a young poet, Robert Finch, whom she supposedly met at Trail Cottage. Yet when I spoke to Professor Finch, now retired from the French department at the University of Toronto, he divulged that he had spent perhaps two hours of his entire life with Mazo de la Roche, back in the early 1920s when he taught at Ridley College in St. Catharines, Ontario. Mr. H.G. Williams, headmaster at Ridley, had introduced the two at an afternoon tea — he gave "lots of encouragement to literary types."

Professor Finch, who remembers Mazo as "a rather taking woman" who "drew you out" (though he adds that he was young and impressionable at the time), emphasizes that Mazo didn't really know him at all. She liked his name, he supposes, for in those days the practice at Ridley was to call one by one's surname. Still, Robert Finch told me an anecdote that is wonderfully apropos of the Whiteoaks. Headmaster Williams, lover of the arts and friend to artists, supported his young teacher in setting up a poetry-writing class. One day, the headmaster received a note from the parents of one of the boys in the poetry group, named Turner, telling him that they already had one poet in the family, and wished to withdraw their son from class.

We might juxtapose this story and an exchange that takes place in *Finch's Fortune* between Renny and Wakefield Whiteoak, the oldest and youngest of the five brothers of the third generation. Wakefield has admitted to writing poetry, which strikes Renny as being "too bad to be true," given the fate of their brothers Eden and Finch, the two artists in the family. Renny tells Wakefield that music and poetry have brought his brothers "nothing but trouble," concluding, "Now, Wake, do you want to be like those two, or like Piers and me? I know we're not artistic or anything of that sort. Intellectual ladies don't get hysterical over us. But we're normal chaps. We've good digestions, good nerves, and healthy appetites." In this novel, where Renny would like to "knock some of the effeminacy" out of Arthur Leigh, and where the "he-men," Renny and Piers, dominate the clan, Eden and Finch find themselves members of their own Dead Poets Society. To Eden, Finch is "the peculiar flower of our peculiar flock," the "final flourish" and perhaps even the justification of the Whiteoaks. Looking back on her maternal forbears, Maisie Roche must have felt the same about herself. She had *earned* the de la Roche patronymic, she had *earned* this trip to Europe, this house in Devon, where her distant ancestors had lived close to the land, mindful of tradition.

Towards the end of the novel, Finch, rebounding from his nervous collapse and the pianist's equivalent of writer's block, returns to Jalna and plays for a full hour before the gathered family. Exactly a year has passed since his twenty-first birthday, the event that opened the narrative, and, to honour the twenty-second anniversary of his birth, Piers and Pheasant name their newborn second son after him. He has loved, he has gone down into the ashes . . . and he has managed to spend the better part of his legacy. In the future, Finch determines, every remaining cent will be spent upon his art. Mazo thus draws to a close what she conceived of as an artist-figure trilogy. In *Jalna*, *Whiteoaks of Jalna*, and *Finch's Fortune*, she had explored the tension between freedom and responsibility, and the alienation and despair of the artist — or any marginalized person — in a hostile environment. Together, these novels constitute a spiritual biography, a by-no-means-completed quest.

Lark Ascending

Lark Ascending, written mainly at Seckington, is an anomaly in the de la Roche canon, an attempt at international fiction, a genre developed by nineteenth-century American writers to dramatize the confrontation between Old and New World values. Mazo's international novel, published in 1932, was composed in the twilight of this literary phase, long after it had reached its zenith in the fictions of Henry James, though Edith Wharton was still actively mining transatlantic themes, *The Gods Arrive* appearing the same year.

The critical response to *Lark Ascending* was, from the beginning, fairly tepid. Like Wharton's novels of the period, it was viewed as magazine fiction; yet it is certainly not without its merits. Again, this novel is of particular interest because it reveals the extent to which Mazo wrote her own life into the circumstances of her characters. Closely resembling an earlier short story, "Quartet" (which was indeed magazine material), published in *Harper's Bazaar* in 1930, *Lark Ascending* draws upon Mazo and Caroline's Continental travels. Both stories have a Massachusetts connection, reflecting their stay in Rockport in the summer of 1927 — Mazo, awaiting the publication of *Jalna*, chose the town partly for its proximity to the offices of Little, Brown in Boston. And both narratives have Italian settings. *Lark Ascending* draws on the time Mazo and Caroline spent in Taormina, Sicily (called Tramontana in the novel), where they stayed for eleven weeks, during which time Mazo celebrated her fiftieth birthday. The cousins then proceeded to Sorrento, Capri, and Naples (setting of "Quartet").

Lark Ascending also resembles "Quartet" in that it focuses on four characters. Two are introduced in Saltport (Rockport), with a Latin lover and a Russian cosmopolite rounding out the cast in the Old World. Mazo's publishers felt some trepidation about her presentation of New Englanders; this was openly expressed by Edward Weeks, her editor at Little, Brown and a Harvard man. In particular, Weeks worried about the ancestry of the novel's heroine, Fay Palmas, whose Indian heritage, through her great-grandmother, struck him as incompatible with regional history. Mazo's concession was to create for Fay's ancestress a Hudson Bay background, one of only two Canadian allusions in the novel (anomalous in itself).

Mazo assuaged her publishers' fears by making her New Englanders individuals rather than types. Yet she conformed to the international novel's presentation of the New England conscience, albeit in her Saltporters the moral vigour and idealism of the past is somewhat diluted. Fay and her nineteen-year-old son Diego, are tangential to this tradition; Diego has some Portuguese blood, and his mother's background is aboriginal. The New England moral character is primarily assigned to a cousin, Josie Froward (whose orphaned state should immediately alert us to her affinity with Caroline Clement), and Fay's upright suitor, Purley Bond, a man of old New England stock.

Once Mazo conveys her quartet across the Atlantic and introduces the impecunious Italian nobleman Conte Gian Montleone, we have all the trappings of international fiction, especially when Fay marries the count. There are already discrepancies between Mazo's novel and its prototypes, however, for Fay is an impostor, not an American heiress but a self-made woman who has spent her adult life baking bread in Saltport. Nevertheless, she becomes entangled in the usual web of Old World deceit and corruption. When Diego's Russian girlfriend, Varvara Wolkonsky, is discovered sharing moonlit caresses with the count, Diego — a mildly passionate pilgrim-cum-artist in the tradition of Hawthorne's Kenyon in *The Marble Faun* and James's Roderick Hudson — is thankful that he has managed to preserve his virginity in the face of Varvara's physical advances. Fay histrionically retreats from the playing field, and Josie and Purley find that they have been in love with each other all along, and return to Massachusetts.

While it may seem that Mazo has simply inverted (and debased) the narrative structure of James's *The Golden Bowl*, she has actually treated her characters in a manner that is clearly self-referential. That Josie applies the finishing touches to her cousin Diego's canvasses suggests Caroline's participation in Mazo's writing; thus Diego's growing resentment of his cousin's artistic collaboration is not without autobiographical implications. Also, Fay is a singer who, at the beginning of the novel, keeps losing her voice; Mazo, as we have seen, had suffered a six-month writer's block while working on *Whiteoaks of Jalna*. The two women "of nearly fifty" who appear in the final chapter, making their first visit to Europe, find the sight of Fay Palmas, who has remained in Sicily, highly romantic. Contessa Fay, dressed in black, has a graceful bearing and a melancholy face; she now seems to believe her own fictions, telling the women that she speaks a bit of English and once made "a little visit" to New England.

Along the same lines, Mazo has imposed her own themes on the framework of the international novel. Faye has "something animal," a second sight, in her; her voice is like a lark's. She slaves for years in her first husband's bakery, and sells the establishment upon his death in order to "spread her wings" in Europe. (How often Mazo associated freedom with flight!) Fay loves watching the French sailors on their ship, "free and unrepressed and bold," and becomes a subject of speculation herself because of "her height, her long, swinging walk, her swarthy skin, arched brows and brilliant eyes." Mazo's self-referentiality and thematic concerns come together when Fay considers how much safer she feels "when bulwarked by fiction." "[T]ruth," we are told, is "congenitally distasteful to her." Fay has a "primitive determination not to allow conventions to deprive her of this romantic escape." Waking in the morning in the count's Villa Benedittini, she feels "extravagantly unreal."

While much of *Lark Ascending* is derivative — at one point Varvara delivers a speech to Fay about New World ignorance of the Old World that seems straight out of Wharton's *The Custom of the Country* — it tells us as much about its author as any of her fiction. Perhaps the (postmodern) way to read the novel is to see Mazo as drawing upon, while subverting, the conventions of international fiction, inscribing her own feelings of social and sexual marginality into the text, and emphasizing the instinctive life over the manners that are so critical to the genre. In the last analysis, *Lark Ascending* is less an exploration of the New England conscience or differences between the Old and New Worlds than it is a dramatization of the inner life of Mazo de la Roche.

FIGURE 12

The Rectory, Hawkchurch, which was the setting of *Beside a Norman Tower*.

FIGURE 13

Mazo and Caroline Clement revisiting Rochedale in 1934. The photograph is inscribed to Dora and Hugh Eayrs, "with our love."

The Faults and Virtues of Her Sex

In April 1931, Mazo's two adopted children, originally named Patty and Michael, arrived at Seckington. The official story passed on by Mazo and Caroline was that they were brother and sister, the orphaned children of friends whom they had met in Italy. That two unmarried women were able to adopt children in England during the 1930s is, to say the least, odd; but then Mazo was aided by Daniel MacMillan, her English publisher, and, according to rumour, his brother Harold, the statesman who became prime minister in 1957. This is one of those mysteries in Mazo's life that will likely never be unravelled, the adoption having been effected in such high and guarded places. The children were renamed René and Esmée. In the custom of the times, they were not encouraged to pursue the question of their parentage beyond what their mother (Mazo) and aunt (Caroline) told them. An indication of their confusion on this score is that when Ronald Hambleton interviewed them in the 1960s, Esmée spoke of René as her brother, while he denied their blood relation, suggesting that there was "a connection" between them. René added that when he approached Caroline about the matter after Mazo's death, he was told that if his adoptive mother had wanted him to know such details, she'd have told him. "We do not know who we are," he unemotionally stated.

Seckington proved impractical for two toddlers — Esmée was two and a half, René thirteen months — so in the autumn the family moved to The Rectory in Hawkchurch, Devon, the setting of *Beside a Norman Tower* (1934). This autobiographical work, which can only be called a fiction because Mazo changed the characters' names, was followed in 1937 by *The Very House*, which documents the period from 1934 to 1935 when the children lived in seaside accommodation and two houses — The Very House in Worplesden, Surrey, and the house *she* called The Very House, though it was actually called The Winnings, and was near Malvern. Between the periods covered by the two books, Mazo and Caroline took a house in London and then transported the children and their nanny back to Canada, where they stayed at Springfield Farm in Erindale until Caroline first was injured in an automobile accident and *then* broke her leg. The family retreated to Castle Frank Road in Toronto for the winter.

In *Beside a Norman Tower*, the children are named Gillian and Diggory, while Mazo is Mother, and Caroline is Karen. Their story is told in the present tense. Mazo is thus able to capture, in an intimate and immediate way, a consciousness divorced from that of her readers. This technique, complemented by her richly expressive use of figurative language, which links the children to the animal and vegetable worlds, is what saves the narrative from becoming merely another cloying tale of happy domesticity, though at times one has the feeling that in writing about her young charges Mazo developed a shortsightedness characteristic of most parents, an inability to realize that one's children are not as interesting to the outside world as they are to oneself. By writing such a fiction, because she had also chosen to publish *The Thunder of New Wings* in *Chatelaine* in 1932, she was running the risk, as well, of being stereotyped as a "ladies' writer" in an era when this label invited a devaluation of literary merit and artistic integrity.

The Very House is less successful, because it lacks the technical virtuosity of Mazo's other autobiographical narratives, *Portrait of a Dog* and *Beside a Norman Tower*. The third-person point of view and use of the past tense distance the reader, and the usual Mazoian tropes (for once) are hardly in evidence. The only break in the monotony is the play Mazo inserted into the text, a play in which Gillian and Diggory perform. It is an interesting blurring of genre.

Beneath the sometimes saccharine surface of these stories is, however, the same dark force that periodically erupts in Mazo's account of her childhood in *Ringing the Changes*. In *Beside a Norman Tower*, for example, David the Persian cat is poisoned, and the appearances he makes prior to Mazo's detailed descriptions of his suffering (his actual death takes place offstage) generally have something sinister about them: his breast is as white as the new gravestones in the churchyard beneath the Norman tower; his prey frequently dangles from his jaws. The post-Darwinian undertones David brings to the text find fuller expression in *The Sacred Bullock and Other Stories of Animals*, a collection Mazo published at the end of the decade. The reader finds Mazo's claim that she didn't read other writers' animal fiction hard to believe, given the similarities between her efforts and Charles G.D. Roberts's disturbing tales of the wilderness.

The angst she embeds beneath the surface cuteness of Gillian and Diggory's world is likely to register with postmodern sensibilities. The sudden appearance of a car, for example, always frightens the children, sending them scuttling like rabbits (the gamekeepers poison David because he hunts rabbits). However, Mazo's constant dwelling on the absolute differences between little boys and girls is today almost guaranteed to annoy — until one senses the pain behind her insistence. Diggory discovers his fellowship with the workmen who serve Mummie and Karen. Someday he will perform manly labours; Gillian, however, will never be a man. When the fishermen turn the capstan, their muscular shoulders moving beneath their jerseys, Gillian sees their activity as a picture, but Diggory sees himself *doing* these things. Yet when Gillian attends dance classes, Diggory looks down at her, albeit from Nurse's arms, "with masculine envy and disapproval" (*Beside a Norman Tower*). Though she is an extremely independent young lady, Gillian eventually succumbs to her family's conditioning: when, for example, she sees distressed women motorists, she concludes that men are better drivers, to which her brother adds, "They've been driving longer. Men were made before women" (*Very House*). And when Diggory celebrates his fifth birthday, he receives a shiny, child-sized motorcar that he knows how to steer and handle by instinct; when Gillian is finally permitted to drive it, she is "in a quiver of nerves," shrieking "Save me! Save me!" as she speeds towards the lily pond: "She was a girl! A woman! 'With all the faults and virtues of the sex!' cried Mummie, embracing her."

Finally, when Diggory cries, he is simply a "male baby in distress." But when Gillian cries, "she asks no comfort. She does not want to be touched. She is alone in her grief. As she averts her face, as you see her quivering mouth, her streaming blue eyes, hear the moaning sobs that shake her, something in you is hurt. You realize that one day she will be a woman" (*Beside a Norman Tower*).

FIGURE 14

René and Esmée in southwestern England in the 1930s.

The Renny Novels

The Jalna novels of the mid-1930s ostensibly belong to Renny. According to the Reverend C.H. Stone, who was locum tenens at Hawkchurch Parish Church at the time Mazo and family lived in The Rectory, Renny was (as he put it in a letter to Hambleton) "the favourite character of nearly all English women who read the books"; during the period Mazo spent in England that culminated in the success of her play *Whiteoaks* in 1936, she produced several Whiteoak novels catering to that preference. *The Master of Jalna* appeared in 1933, and *Young Renny* in 1935, with *Whiteoak Harvest* following the opening of the play. In focusing on Renny, Mazo strengthened her archetypal association of the Whiteoaks with the instinctive forces of nature, captured through tropes that link family members to the animal and vegetable kingdoms. Nowhere is this relation more pronounced than within Jalna's master himself.[4]

As chieftain of his clan, Renny most fully embodies the mythical associations of the Whiteoak name. Not only does the second chapter of *The Master of Jalna* bear the title "Family Tree," but also, symbolically, Renny appears in an oak grove astride a horse on the dustjacket. As a consummate equestrian, he is equally affiliated with the animal kingdom. We are told that "His association with horses, his familiarity with the saddle, his long years of responsibility, had marked him"; Renny's feet are "more at home in the stirrups than on the ground," and Alayne notices how her husband's head is set on his shoulders "like the head of a thoroughbred." Robert Bly has argued in *Iron John* that "The horse, when contrasted with its rider, reminds men and women of the animal side of human beings, and of the body. The rider stands for the intelligence or intellect or mind, and the horse stands for the animal desires and instincts and energies that have their home there." Appropriately, Renny and his mount seem so unified that, to Alayne, the spiritual and animal in Renny cannot be separated. Furthermore, Renny's identification with Reynard the Fox of medieval anthropomorphic beast epics, a figure whose story is rooted in Aesop's fables of the sixth century B.C., invests Old Redhead with the archetypal cunning essential to his role as chieftain. As Mazo's exemplar of instinctive life, Renny is closely allied to Bly's Wildman, whose law runs in the underground (in the Iron John legend he lies at the bottom of a pond) and whose qualities include "love of spontaneity, association with wildness, and respect for riskiness."

In drawing upon the fantasy life of the Play, developed from her childhood dream, Mazo had tapped the collective unconscious, that dark wellspring — or bottomless pond — that was the source of her imaginative power. In *The Master of Jalna*, she continued to confront the demons within this buried world through the lives of her characters. The character who most poignantly serves as authorial persona is Pauline Lebraux, whose "passionately unchildlike" love for her father is transferred to Renny at the time of Lebraux's death. Possessing her creator's tall, pale, straight-legged appearance, Pauline also shares her predispositions, proclaiming, "I think men are wonderful!", then throwing herself into her surrogate father's arms during a thunderstorm. Her tormented eyes fixed upon Renny, she confesses between sobs, "Oh, I love you — I love you — I can't help it — but I love you so terribly," and indicates that she wants to make love to him, though she also acknowledges that this is "wicked." Here we see Mazo, for all her expressed aversion to modern psychology, toying with an Electra complex. This is reinforced when Pauline vents her anger towards her mother, Clara:

> So this was the sort of woman Renny — if he had been going to love either of them — would have preferred to her!
>
> She remembered the frequent quarrels between her father and mother, how she had always passionately, in her own mind, taken her father's side, even when she had been too young to understand what the quarrel was about. A wild anger against Clara rose in her, filled her heart to bursting. She hated her in that moment.

Yet Pauline's is by no means the only voice encoding the author's.

Eden Whiteoak, whose impending death is at the heart of the novel, despises what he sees as the feminine in himself: "He felt a strain of femineity in himself, a careless treachery, a power of appeal, and he hated these qualities." And then there is Sarah Court Leigh, who becomes Finch's wife after her husband's drowning. She confesses, "I am no good at mixing with other people. Especially other women." At this point, one recalls Mazo's personal aversion to large gatherings and her preference for the company of men, aspects of her mother's personality that Esmée Rees still mentions.

Plot development in *The Master of Jalna* further suggests its psychodramatic underpinnings. If Arthur Leigh's drowning in the St. Lawrence symbolizes his inability to connect to the instinctive life (represented by bodies of water in Mazo's writing), Renny's actions imply that he errs in the opposite direction; he is cursed by what Alayne Archer sees as "a devouring instinct." By the end of *The Master of Jalna*, it has become apparent that Renny, lacking the self-control that comes with reason, has relinquished the reins of authority. Using Jalna as security, he borrows money from Sarah; when Aunt Augusta learns that her nephew has mortgaged the ancestral home, she dies of a stroke. Renny needs the money to set up a household for the Lebraux women, but his generosity can no longer pass for altruism when he makes love to Clara Lebraux on a bed of pine needles while his wife maintains a lonely vigil at Jalna. And, earlier in the novel, Renny's insistence that his ailing brother perform farmwork for his room and board leads to Eden's death from tubercular haemorrhaging.

Although Finch is not as prominent in *The Master of Jalna* as *Finch's Fortune*, he is, in fact, in the process of becoming lord of the manor. His marriage to Sarah is insurance against Jalna's being taken from the Whiteoaks, and his growing maturity as both pianist and composer will bring financial stability to an estate that Renny has allowed to fall into disrepair, both literally and figuratively. Mazo presents Renny's charismatic power as masking his neglect of family and reason, and this clearly reflects the author's ambivalent feelings towards her father, the charming overgrown boy in his buckskin hunting jacket with yet another dog at his side. At the same time, by having Finch meet his destiny as the "flower of his flock," Mazo implies her own personal sense of artistic accomplishment, her successful discharge of those responsibilities conventionally assigned to men.

Yet when she submitted *Young Renny* to her publishers, she was abruptly reminded that however spectacular her successes, the book world was still masculine territory. Mazo was deeply hurt and angered upon discovering that Edward Weeks and Ellery Sedgwick were joining forces to express their dissatisfaction with the novel, which was set in 1906 and was thus the first Whiteoak narrative in which the clock had been turned back. She wrote to Alfred McIntyre, "I am not a machine; I am not even strong. . . . I am now for the first time in my life thoroughly depressed about my work. I even considered the possibility that I have written too much about the Whiteoaks and should write nothing else." Mazo was haunted by criticism that her portrayal of cousin Malahide Court was mere "caricature," that her presentation of Mary Wakefield (Renny's stepmother) was "wooden," and that her treatment of other characters was "watered"; she told her publisher that these adverse comments, expressed while she was still at work on the manuscript, hung over her as she completed the novel. Fortunately, Daniel MacMillan came to her rescue (though we might question in hindsight whether he was actually performing the author a service) by sending the manuscript straight off to the printers, deeming it equal to the earlier Whiteoak novels (qtd. in Hambleton, *Mazo de la Roche*). From this time onward, with one exception, Mazo would alternate her Jalna chronicles between the past and present — sending her manuscripts to London before Boston.

Mazo was not, of course, powerless to respond to what she viewed as an attack upon her literary self-esteem. Threatening to take her writing elsewhere, she quickly caused her American publishers to regret their tactlessness, with Weeks heaping unstinted praise on her next novel, *Whiteoak Harvest*, the story of Renny and Alayne's estrangement and reconciliation. In a letter he wrote to Mazo on Valentine's day 1936, Weeks claimed that the impression the new novel had made upon him was second only to *Jalna*'s. The generally very diplomatic Harvard man waxed poetic: "I think of *Young Renny* as a venture out into the early dawn when even the most familiar outlines are made uncertain and a trace chill. Whereas *Whiteoak Harvest* wears all the golden, mellow tone of an English sunset when light and color combine to give you pictures which cannot be forgotten." Mazo herself clearly placed this sixth Whiteoak novel high in her canon, remarking in *Ringing the Changes* that the *Whiteoak Chronicles* (the 1940 collection of Jalna novels up to and including *Whiteoak Harvest*) represented "the sustained work of a lifetime"; her other books — except *Possession* and *Delight* and the forthcoming *Growth of a Man* and *Quebec: Historic Seaport* — she dismissed as "diversions, distractions."

Mazo made this assessment in describing her feelings about the relationship she enjoyed with her reading public. Yet a good deal of her energy during this period was devoted to the theatre. In helping *Whiteoaks* find its way to the London stage Mazo was moving towards an exhilarating climax to a breathtaking decade.

Whiteoaks *(The Play)*

While Mazo and family had lived at Seckington, Raymond Massey and some fellow actors had suggested that she dramatize *Jalna*; Massey wanted to play Finch. But *Jalna*'s author had not felt ready, in spite of the success of her one-act plays in the 1920s, to tackle the West End. She did, however, write a play based on *Whiteoaks of Jalna* several years later, sending the manuscript to Massey, only to find that he was no longer interested in the part of Finch; still, with his encouragement, she passed the manuscript on to her friend St. John Ervine, whom Mazo had intertextually honoured in *Whiteoaks of Jalna* by having Finch play a role in one of Ervine's plays. Ervine answered that he was "in seventeen minds about it" (*Ringing the Changes*), and so matters stood as Mazo and family left The Rectory for Canada in 1933.

While at Castle Frank Road working on *Young Renny*, Mazo received word that British actress Nancy Price wanted to produce *Whiteoaks* in London, so she and Caroline sailed back to England to work on the script. Upon its completion, Mazo signed a contract, but it would be another two years before *Whiteoaks* was produced. In the interim, *Jalna* was filmed in Hollywood by R.K.O. Productions, and Mazo's response to the result was predictably ambivalent. She and Caroline had seen their very first film only shortly before this time, and while, according to her friends, Mazo demonstrated a surprising interest in television in her later years, she clearly regarded the cinema as a lowbrow threat to imaginative life.

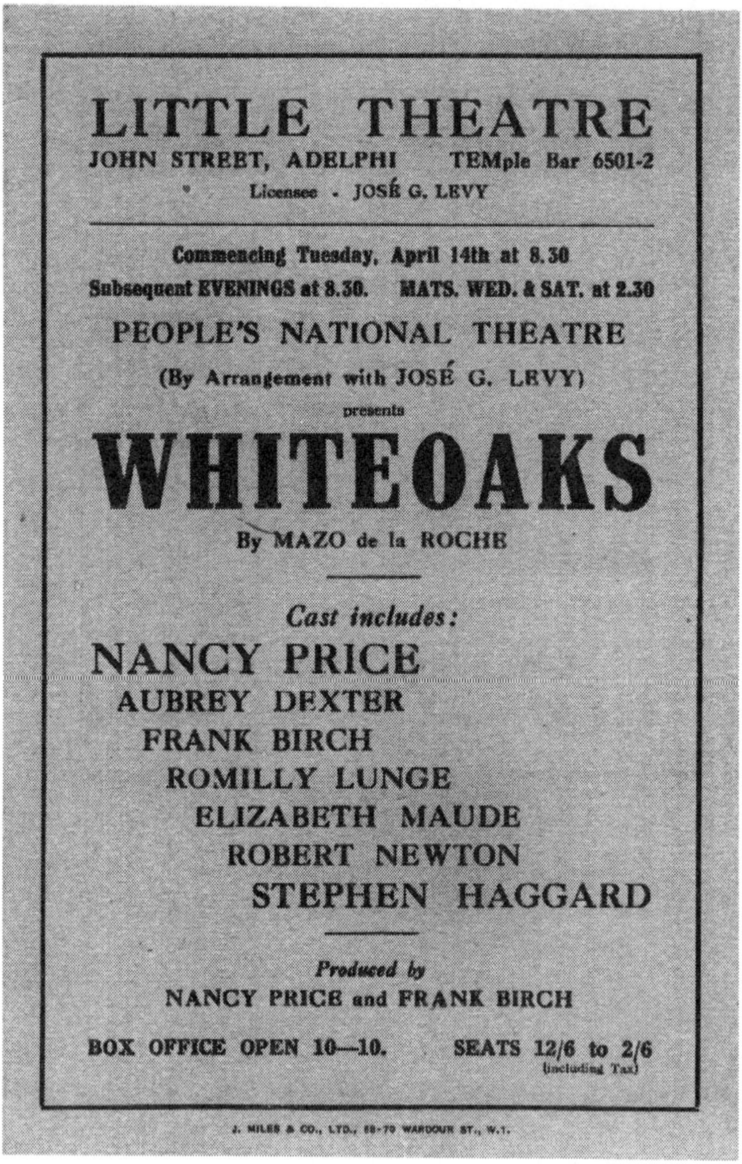

FIGURE 15

Playbill announcing the opening of *Whiteoaks* at London's Little Theatre of the Adelphi, 13 April 1936.

In January 1936 — the month of the deaths of Kipling and George V and of torrential rains in England — Mazo was asked by Nancy Price, who was not only codirecting the production but also acting the role of Gran Whiteoak, to write a new last act. Reestablishing themselves in a house close to Buckingham Palace, in Stafford Place, where Mazo had worked on the play in 1933, the cousins felt the excitement build. Mazo was actively involved in casting (a multitude of parrots auditioned for the part of Boney) and rehearsals.

Whiteoaks, combining the first two Jalna novels, opened on 13 April at the Little Theatre of the Adelphi. Following numerous curtain calls, Mazo — nervously responding to shouts of "Author! Author!" — made a short speech, after which she and Caroline gave a party for over sixty people. The next morning's notices were balm to her soul — Mazo wrote to longtime Canadian friends Anne and Edward Dimock, saying that of the eight daily papers, seven had run favourable reviews (Hambleton, *Mazo de la Roche*). Although Caroline and Nancy Price later expressed widely disparate views on the role Price played in revising the script, it is clear that the final product, which had three acts and only one set, was dramatically different from Mazo's original conception, for her manuscript indicated twelve changes of scene in five acts.

In spite of the glowing notices, the audiences were not large, and after two months there was talk of closing. Then, by chance, Nancy Price was offered the Playhouse Theatre for a couple of weeks. Just before *Whiteoaks* moved there, St. John Ervine published a supportive review coupling the names de la Roche and Chekhov. The same week, George Bernard Shaw dashed off a postcard to Nancy Price complimenting her on her portrayal of the centenarian Adeline Whiteoak. An excerpt from this postcard prominently displayed on the Playhouse's billboard, combined with Ervine's praise and the new locale, did the trick: the play ran for nearly three years, closing in the shadow of impending war after more than eight hundred performances. Mazo was again triumphant.

Watching Boney — who came to be known all over London — steal the last curtain call, spreading his wings in the floodlights to thunderous applause, Maisie Roche must have seen a symbol of her own apotheosis, something commensurate with her own capacity for wonder. People came over and over again to see the play. Queen

Mary made "four or five visits to the play," at least once accompanied by the Dukes of Gloucester, Kent, and Windsor (Hambleton, *Mazo de la Roche*). What more could a descendant of United Empire Loyalists ask, short of high tea in Tory Heaven?

An oft-circulated story about Boney's meeting with the queen perhaps best signifies Mazo's position at this time. At auditions, Nancy Price had looked for the wildest parrot, believing that such a bird would ultimately make the best performer. She settled on a yellow-fronted Amazon, the only problem being that the new Boney hated leather gloves. When the set carpenter was sent to hospital after being attacked by the bird during a training session, Price decided to handle the parrot bare-handed, and from that time on, she became Boney's "trusted friend" (Hambleton, *Mazo de la Roche*). Imagine her consternation, then, when after a performance the white-gloved Queen Mary requested the presence of Gran and Boney, holding out her hand to the feathered celebrity! Yet Boney demurred to the queen's overtures, receiving a kiss, and acquiring one of his biggest fans.

Boney's creator strongly identified with birds. Indeed, another well-known anecdote involves Mazo's response to seagulls in flight above the cliffs of coastal Cornwall: "What a life! To be free, like that!" (qtd. in Hambleton, *Mazo de la Roche*). Boney, however, was not free because his wings had been cut; yet Mazo had created him out of her desire to portray a creature with a furious resistance to control. She worshipped at the shrine of instinct. At the same time, as a daughter of United Empire Loyalists, she venerated tradition. She was part of a generation Timothy Findley described to me as having been raised to think that it had nothing to offer unless its members were "wearing white gloves and standing at attention." Was Mazo, one wonders, ever tempted to attack the symbolic gloved hand? Was she, like the Amazonian parrot, ever fearful of the control that hand exerted? "Be never afraid!" Gran Whiteoak admonished: her dying words closed the play; and Boney, on cue, gave a horrible cry and perched on her shoulder. Mazo spread her wings in the floodlights and accepted the applause.

After touring Britain, *Whiteoaks* headed across the Atlantic, and Ethel Barrymore was engaged to play Gran. Though Mazo much preferred Nancy Price in the role, the play was given a warm welcome in Canada, if it elicited a rather cynical response in New York. At a time when her artistic endeavours commanded royal attention in England, Mazo must have felt her Loyalist homing instincts justified. As early as November 1936, she had, in fact, purchased her first home since Trail Cottage, this time not in the shadow of silver birches but of Windsor Castle.

Growth of a Man

Having found The Winnings, the estate in the Cotswalds where the family had lived since December 1934, too remote from London, and winters in Herefordshire too cold, Mazo and Caroline moved into Vale House, near Windsor, in April 1937. Vale House was about as far removed from Trail Cottage as its proprietor was from Maisie Roche. Sitting on some twenty acres, the Elizabethan manor was replete with orchards, lily pond, greenhouses, and a sunken garden. The house boasted a minstrels' gallery, a conservatory, a ballroom, and an immense schoolroom. That August, Barbara Sayers, now in her seventeenth year, travelled to England to visit her old neighbours. Today, Mrs. Barbara Sayers Larson remembers Vale House as "a delightful, very relaxed, typically English, Tudorish place with a beautiful garden" in which she was served tea from a trolley as René tore across the flagstones on a tricycle "like a mad thing." To her, Mazo remained unchanged from Trail Cottage days, though of course she had, in the meantime, seen Bunty's mistress in her new incarnation as celebrated writer, with Caroline and children in tow, back in Clarkson.

That August, Mazo was hard at work on *Growth of a Man*, which she had started writing within a fortnight of moving into Vale House. Although she had been planning this novel since 1935, it is hardly coincidental that she should have begun writing about Newmarket now that she had decided to put down roots in what she imagined was going to be her permanent home. It must have been odd for her to gaze out the window at Jersey cows in the pasture as she moved through memory to the fields north of Newmarket, to the time when little Maisie Roche would visit Clement and Willson relations on their farms in Innisfil Township, north of Newmarket.

It was in this region that her cousin H.R. (Reggie) MacMillan, on whose life the novel is based, spent his childhood. The first eight chapters of the book, arguably equal to any of her writing, provide an evocative picture of late-nineteenth century rural life in this part of southern Ontario — its hardships, severity, and beauty. Mazo wrote to B.K. Sandwell of *Saturday Night* that *Growth of a Man* was "one of the best things I have done," and in these chapters she realized the promise of a local realism, the seeds of which had distinguished *Possession* and *Delight*. Yet her audience wanted the Whiteoaks, and while critics such as Hugh Eayrs and E.K. Brown lauded Mazo's accomplishment in the *Canadian Bookman*, the author nursed her disappointment at the realization that *Growth of a Man* was only "mildly liked" in Canada (qtd. in Hambleton, *Mazo de la Roche*).

Mazo's closeness to this novel stemmed not only from the pride she took in her craft, but also from the fact that it was a distillation of her early life; for while the narrative is ostensibly based on MacMillan's triumph over extreme adversity, it clearly relates to Mazo's own success story. She stuck to the framework provided by the years of MacMillan's life that preceded his becoming timber-trade minister for the federal government, but in creating her protagonist, Shaw Manifold, she transformed her cousin into a projection of her self.

In her representation of Shaw's childhood, for example, Mazo captures her own sense of isolation in the large Lundy household, for when Shaw's young father, a physician, dies of tuberculosis, his mother is forced to leave him with her parents, whose farmhouse is crowded with those of their thirteen children who have remained unmarried. Shaw, encountering the philistinism of the Gowers, is set apart not only by his age but also by his imagination and longing for an intellectual life.

An ancestral embodiment of the world to which Shaw aspires is his maternal great-grandfather, after whom he is named, a lover of books, beautiful music, and the life of the spirit. Great-grandfather Gower represents, in fact, the familial link between Mazo and Reggie MacMillan: their own great-grandfather, Hiram Robinson

FIGURE 16

The Sharon Temple. Mazo's great-grandfather, after unveiling the golden ball, "sang, in a voice like an angel's, a hymn of dedication" (*Ringing the Changes*).

Willson. The importance of Willson to Mazo's inherited sense of identity is suggested by the disproportionate space accorded to him in the chapter on her maternal forbears in *Ringing the Changes*, a long passage that was lifted almost verbatim from chapter 1 of *Growth of a Man*. In this description of Shaw Gower/Hiram Willson's contribution to the Sharon Temple, a version of Solomon's Temple as envisioned by the charismatic spiritual leader David Willson in the 1820s, Mazo expressed a passionate sense of the past, accenting a blood link to Upper Canada of which she could be justifiably proud. For Hiram Willson had played an integral role in the building of this extraordinary three-storey structure, having unveiled at its opening the golden sphere that crowned it, symbolically situated above a model of the ark.

Shaw's lonely youth is devoted to reading his great-grandfather's books, as romantic to him as the now-deserted temple. They are gateways to the world of intellectual and spiritual integrity. At the same time, under the influence of his great-grandfather, whose books "had opened the door of his imagination," Shaw cultivates an inner life strongly suggestive of the Play, a realm that expands when he finds youthful company with whom to share it. Mazo, who had already assigned a dog-eared copy of *Huckleberry Finn* to Fay Palmas in *Lark Ascending*, obliquely acknowledges Samuel Clemens, that distant relation of Caroline's whose writing celebrates the escapades of boyhood, when she has Shaw and his best friend, Ian Blair, meet with the two Scott brothers in a secret cave (the deserted root house of a neighbouring farm). There they pretend to be pirates, writing out bloodthirsty messages and sharing the spoils of their plunder. Shaw is severely punished for his truancy by Grandma Gower, who combines the roles of *Huckleberry Finn*'s Miss Watson and Mazo's own Mrs. Handsomebody. Furthermore, Shaw's relation to Ian is that of Huck Finn to Tom Sawyer, the former following a no-nonsense philosophy, the latter carried away by his romantic imagination. These attitudes persist beyond childhood: Shaw and his comrades continue to greet each other with pirate code words; Shaw fails to respond to the call of war, arguing that he's interested not in destruction but in building up, yet Ian and the Scotts leap, Tom Sawyer-like, at the opportunity to distinguish themselves in heroic battle. The brothers die in World War I.

Had Reggie MacMillan chosen to read *Growth of a Man* (he claimed not to have, and his wife reportedly said she disliked the novel), he might have raised his eyebrows at his cousin's importation of the Play into his boyhood, but he would most certainly have been astonished to discover the homoerotic undercurrent that is never far from the surface of this Bildungsroman. The object of most of this libidinous energy is Jack Searle, a neighbouring farmhand who befriends young Shaw. First encountered waist-high in water (a tip-off for any seasoned Mazoite), the naked Searle is a monument to his creator's sexually infused paganism; he is "one of those superbly made creatures which Nature sometimes wastefully tosses into a class where beauty is no asset." Fascinated by Searle's profanities and what is later described as his "queer beauty," Shaw quickly undresses and plunges into the pool. His odyssey involves a series of encounters with Searle, who, after robbing the Gowers and eloping with the daughter of his employer, heads to the frontier under another name. Each time Searle appears, Mazo exhibits her fascination with his beautiful body, breathlessly detailing, for example, the saturnalian movements he makes as he dances, and, later, describing how he is given a shave by a rough companion on a launch (Huck and Jim's raft), "his muscular legs sprawling, his shirt open at the throat disclosing his fine bronzed chest, his golden head thrown back and his face upturned to the razor."

During most of Shaw's young manhood, he is divided between his love for other men and his devotion to his mother, as intense a devotion as that which Mazo expresses towards her own father in *Ringing the Changes*. In addition to Searle's companionship, there is Ian Blair's: "To find themselves close together again made them, for the first time, conscious of love between them"; "Now, thrown together in the lonely forest, their emotions were intensified. They felt that they wished they might never be separated again"; "Shaw seemed to have eyes only for Ian."

H.R. MacMillan, after a two-and-a-half-year bout with tuberculosis brought on by the rigours of his life in the outdoors, married. And so Shaw, emerging from a Quebec sanitorium, weds Ian's sister, Elspeth. Though his discovery of his inner warrior through his heroic struggle to live restores the focus of the novel, paving the way for Shaw to set up house with Elspeth *and* his mother, the intensity of the narrative is proportionate to the author's expression of her inner life (the effects of isolation in childhood, adolescent sexual longings, the emotional bonds between offspring and parent). When Shaw ventures into the terra incognita of the American South and British Columbia, the narrative languishes. Still, *Growth of a Man* is a generally dynamic if occasionally bizarre grafting of one life onto another.

The most revealing aspect of the novel is the way Mazo presents an ambitious girl who, in attempting to escape from the village of Thorriton, where she and Shaw attend school, is also rejecting the role she has been assigned by the community. This girl is named Louie Adams (a neuter name, like Mazo's), and she is Shaw's greatest academic rival — he roughs her up when she claims superiority. Later, when Louie attempts to equal an athletic feat of Shaw's, their mutual animosity again flares. She asks him what he's going to be when he grows up:

"Oh, I don't know yet. Perhaps a doctor. But anyhow something a long way from here. I'm going to do something out in the world."

"So am I."

"You couldn't. You're only a girl."

She hung her head.

Yet Louie does indeed do something out in the world: she escapes to New York City and finds work in a beauty parlour. She powders her skin, darkens her eyelashes, and gets a permanent wave.

But Thorriton will be avenged, and when Shaw travels to the sanitorium in Quebec, he finds that Louie is one of its patients, and that she is hopelessly in love with him (she has always been) and terminally ill. Like Mazo at the time of her breakdown, Louie expresses a wish to become Roman Catholic — to "feel safer" — and, baptized and confirmed, she receives her last Communion from a priest with his own foot in the grave. Shaw, on the road to recovery, determines to forget his old rival, "who had now become for him the symbol of death, yet in that death possessed of a feverish life." Louie's inner warrior fails to deliver. Shaw, on the other hand, returns to the game. The old boys of the pirate days greet each other in front of their wives with, *"Blood on your brow, brother. There are bloody deeds to be done."* Mazo returned to the deeds of the Whiteoaks . . . and to Canada.

Into the War Years

In spite of Caroline's veneration of British values and Mazo's insistence that, had World War II not intervened, the family would have remained at Vale House, their voyage from Liverpool to Boston on 1 April 1939 marked the end of their English days. With the exception of a five-month sojourn in New England brought to an end by the war, the cousins were entering a period of repatriation, and René and Esmée were about to become Canadian children. Prior to their departure from England, Mazo had, in fact, confessed to Edward Weeks (who found them a house in Beacon Hill opposite his own) that Windsor no longer agreed with her, that she felt a deep longing for Canada. Though she loved Vale House more than any other house they had known or were to know, Mazo had recently had a cyst removed from her windpipe, and her precarious health, coupled with Hitler's speeches on the wireless, convinced her that the time had come to return home.

She recalls in her autobiography that, during this period, she tried to shut the terrible events on the Continent out of her mind by living in the world of *Whiteoak Heritage*, which she had begun in October 1938. But the British government was distributing gas masks and advising all citizens to store food and water, and it therefore became impossible even for Mazo, with her determinedly escapist nature, to ignore grim reality. *Ringing the Changes*, published twelve years after the war's end, concludes with the family's return to North America: "I feel no urge to write of my life during the years of the War or after. Each of us lives through several lives in his time. This latest period of mine is mostly a record of books written, of seeing my children grow up, of seeing a different sort of world rise into my astonished view." If Mazo was forced to bow to the exigencies of the actual world, she could still manipulate the plot of her own story. And it is clear that she regarded her life after the 1930s as an anticlimax.

By the time *Whiteoak Heritage* was finished, in June of 1940, Mazo and family had settled in a house that her Uncle Walter Lundy had found for them north of Toronto in what is today the city of North York. Back then, the area at Bayview and Steeles Avenues was remote from Toronto. Windrush Hill, their new abode, was, in fact, an old farmhouse. To it Mazo's architect made impressive additions, including an east wing housing an oak-panelled library with a beautiful mullioned window, a reproduction of Mazo's study at Vale House. Today Windrush Hill, which Mazo also called Singing Pines, is the temple of the Zoroastrian Society of Ontario, whose members undoubtedly have a less nostalgic view of English colonialism; the pseudo-Elizabethan window has been torn out to make room for an altar.

Like *Growth of a Man*, *Whiteoak Harvest* represents a leap across the chasm of time, in this instance to Bronte and Oakville. Set in the period immediately following World War I, it begins with the homecoming of Sergeant Maurice Vaughan and Captain Renny Whiteoak. In introducing a divided house into the third chapter, Mazo was recalling a time in her own life, which she had already evoked in *Portrait of a Dog*. In this incarnation, the divided house contains, on one side, the object of Renny's desires, a sexy tomboy, Chris Dayborn, dressed in khaki breeches and open-necked shirt, whose pretend brother, Jim, is really her husband; and, on the other side, listening through paper-thin walls, an "older woman, Mrs. Stroud," who moves predatorily from Renny's young stepbrother Eden to his sexagenarian Uncle Ernest, though it's really Old Redhead she's after.

Turning the clock back to the days at Rochedale Farm when Pierre Mansbendel had left their relationship in limbo, prior to establishing a union with Aunt Eva, Mazo vilifies Amy Stroud, the fairy-tale ogress, by having her turn the hot-blooded symbol of Renny's masculinity, his horse, Launceton, out into the freezing cold. Like the Roches' Johnny, the chestnut who was let out by a stableboy, Launceton ruptures himself in a snowdrift. There is, however, one positive outcome to Launceton's death: the departure of the snakelike Mrs. Stroud (of whom the ordinarily indomitable

Renny remains afraid). But then Amy Stroud never really belonged to the Whiteoak demesne in the first place; Gran makes the same remark about her — a social condemnation worthy of Galsworthy's Forsytes — that other members of the clan will later apply to Clara Lebraux. She isn't "out of the top drawer."

The divided house as a symbol pertains not only to Mazo's general opposition of instinct and repression but also, more explicitly, to matters of sexual preference and frustration. In *A Boy in the House*, written a decade later, a male writer experiences a secret passion for a slender boy (whom readers observe, as they do Fawnie and Jack Searle, naked in water). In this divided house, a thin wall divides Mazo's artist figure from the lad and his employers, two elderly, shabby-genteel sisters. The tale, which has a Gothic atmosphere, redolent with decay — there is a rank garden, "worm-poisoned fruit," a rotting woodshed — is propelled by the homoerotic encounters between the tormented writer and the object of his "almost overpowering attraction." The tension finally explodes in violence between the two women, "strange, sensitive, neurotic creatures." When one of them murders the other, the boy takes the blame, and the story ends with his physical incarceration, though it is the writer who is trapped inside his own longings.

Clearly Mazo viewed civilization as following the same destructive course — denial and repression ending in violence. *Wakefield's Course* (1941) takes the surviving Whiteoak brothers — Renny, Piers, Finch, and Wakefield — away from the protective walls of Jalna and into the madness that lies beyond. The first half of the novel is fuelled by the heady excitement precipitated by the triumph of the play *Whiteoaks* on the London stage: Wakefield, Finch, and Sarah are living in Gayfere Street (not far from St. James Park) when Wake lands a part in a play to be performed at a "small but not obscure" theatre off the Strand. Parallels between the novel and Mazo's personal experience abound. The actors have a rehearsal in the club room of the Foreign Waiters' Association (the Swiss Waiters' Club of *Ringing the Changes*); on opening night, the playwright reluctantly bows to cries of "Author! Author!" and then finds his way to the stage, where he makes "a really brilliant speech but he [speaks] so low that only the members of the orchestra [hear] it." A large party in the house in Gayfere Street follows the performance, and all but two of the next morning's reviews are favourable. The production moves to a larger theatre. Finally, its success, like that of *Whiteoaks*, is seen to be "one of those mysteries of the theatre which no one can solve."

But, as Mazo learned when her play attained tremendous success, the joy that such a triumph can generate is fleeting. Chaos erupts in the microcosm and the macrocosm: Wakefield discovers that the actress playing opposite him, with whom he has fallen in love, is none other than Renny's illegitimate daughter, Molly Griffith, the product of his half-brother's affair with Chris Dayborn, the androgynous tomboy of the divided house (like homosexuality, incest is never far from the surface of the Whiteoak novels, with brothers seducing and marrying each other's wives, and girls falling in love with their substitute fathers). By this point in the chronicles, Pauline Labraux has found an antidote to her Renny fixation — the convent; now Wakefield escapes from the source of *his* sorrows, moving from inner to outer chaos, by enlisting in the R.A.F. as the war inexorably advances upon the Whiteoaks and all they represent.

The ending of the novel is equally contrived. Reminding us that there are, indeed, alternatives to the overt masculinity of Renny and Piers, the author has the artists of the family, Finch the musician and Wakefield the actor, participate in a daring operation during the Dunkirk evacuation. They rescue the wounded Renny (never too old for martial glory) and ferry him to a hospital ship. Wakefield instantly forgives Renny his transgressions, pillowing the family chieftain's head on his knee. Old Redhead doesn't even seem to find it especially odd that Wake and Finch have managed to spot him in the midst of three hundred thousand evacuating soldiers simply by means of his unusual hair colour. His greeting to his half-brothers is "Hullo, kids."

While British readers were clearly hungry for such heroism, the American public was, apparently, less voracious. Mazo's next fiction, an implausible story of two boys — one American and one English — switched at the time of birth, was rejected by Little, Brown. Filled with references to Dunkirk and the sinking of the *Royal Oak*, *The Two Saplings* (1942) builds to a patriotic climax when the American boy — who has been raised in the Cotswalds by the English parents of the baby with whom he has been exchanged — is brought to the safety of New England by his biological parents, yet chooses to return to England to fight in the war. Regardless of his birthright, Mazo's young American obeys a summons from his heart, the call of the trumpet borne across the Atlantic. Perhaps Little, Brown objected more to the preposterous plot than to the author's uncomplimentary presentation of the American mother; yet Mazo's anti-American, Loyalist sentiments were never more prominently in the foreground, and after the war she would become increasingly resistant to what she saw as the onslaught of American materialism and mass culture.

Quebec: Historic Seaport

During the war years, Mazo also accepted a commission from Doubleday to contribute to its Seaport Series. She wrote a history of Quebec, while Stephen Leacock wrote one of Montreal; thus these two icons of Canadian literature share more than the same churchyard. What is most striking about Mazo's *Quebec: Historic Seaport* (1944) is the affinity it demonstrates between her methodology and today's historiography, for not only does she render Quebec's story as narrative, forgoing notes and bibliography, but she also attacks history's so-called objectivity. Observing, in her preface to the book, that greater historians than herself openly contradict each other, she concludes: "In truth, it has been one of my difficulties to choose between entirely opposite versions of the same event."

When Ronald Hambleton suggested in an interview that she had written her life into her books, Mazo challenged him to find anything of herself in this history of Quebec City. Yet today, much of the book's interest is in exactly what she denied, in what it reveals about its author. Confessing that while writing the book she was in danger of becoming a bore to her family as she would regale them with stories of persecution and torture, Mazo directs us to her study's most salient feature — its obsessive record of cruelty, barbarism, and mutilation. (Hambleton later elicited René's memories of this time.

René recalled that his mother put the family off their meals with her gruesome stories of scalpings and other tortures, tales that had no effect upon *Mazo's* appetite.) Indeed, in constructing her narrative Mazo seems never to have missed an opportunity to describe the New World savagery witnessed by such legends as Champlain, Talon, Frontenac, Montcalm, and Levis, though their collaboration in these brutalities generally receives short shrift. That the English and French butchered each other on the battlefield is part of the natural order of things, but when the Natives creep out of the woods to scalp the very soldiers who have embroiled them in these conflicts, we feel that our stomachs are meant to churn.

And they do! Mazo seems to revel in the sadism of these scenes. That she had a cruel streak buried within her own nature is suggested not only by these vivid accounts, but also by her creation of Dennis Whiteoak, son of Finch, who emerges in the next decade as a monster child every bit as savage as Mazo's historical dramatis personae. Ellery Sedgwick commented on this repressed side of Mazo's nature, citing a passage in *Ringing the Changes* where Mazo describes removing a thorn an inch and a half long embedded in the eye of her Scottie, Moulin. The reader in no way questions how traumatic this was for Moulin's mistress, but the passage displays a preoccupation with cruelty that connects her fictional and nonfictional writing, and a deep abhorrence of pain and suffering as well as a morbid fascination with them.

In *Quebec*, this morbidity results in what we might call the eroticism of the grotesque, if we think of the grotesque as involving exaggeration and distortion, violence and physical abnormality. Mazo's grotesque imagery actually foregrounds the story being told. Long after we've forgotten the essential narrative of this history of a seaport, we still remember the British commander being torn in two by a cannon ball, Native warriors drinking warm blood for courage, captives being mutilated and roasted, the scenes of torture in which the covert and frustrated sexuality behind the act is palpable.

Yet this book is not without humour. When the New England fleet of Sir William Phipps is routed by the Canadians and encounters further disasters sailing back to Boston, Mazo tells us, "Governor Bradstreet of Massachusetts wrote: 'Shall our Father spit in our face and we be not ashamed?' " She then adds, "Which seems to credit the Almighty with rather bad manners, to say the least of it." Nor does she waste her data. Having established that Sir William's mother gave birth to twenty-one sons and five daughters, Mazo remarks of the commander's return to Boston harbour, "It is interesting to picture Phipp's greeting from his twenty-five brothers and sisters."

Mazo's problem in writing this book was, by her own admission, keeping her "very active imagination in leash." The result may not be great history, but it is certainly compelling narration, calculated to entertain the popular audience for whom the Seaport Series was intended. And if, occasionally, Mazo can't help allowing her Loyalist sympathies to prejudice her account — as they do when she revels in Sir Guy Carleton's contempt for those officers of the American revolutionary forces who had been butchers and innkeepers (Acton House is, of course, forgotten!) — we can at least console ourselves that *this* historian is not even pretending to be neutral.

Chief Mourner

Ronald Hambleton concluded that Mazo de la Roche was "the chief mourner for the dying English influence in Canada." Yet Mazo's writing mourned far more than the abandonment of English ways; indeed, the publication of *The Building of Jalna* in 1944 ushered in the final phase of the Whiteoak chronicles, the author's lament for a lost nation. Mazo began to realize that she was living in a world where the old landmarks were disappearing and the road signs had been systematically turned upside down.

The Building of Jalna goes back to the genesis of the Whiteoak saga, the arrival of Captain Philip Whiteoak, his wife, and infants at the "perfect paradise" of the Loyalist social vision. As Dennis Duffy has noted, from the beginning Mazo had split the Loyalist myth in the Jalna novels to produce "a more genteel variation," and in *The Building of Jalna* this division is personified by the Whiteoaks, who are not Loyalists but represent a Loyalist ideal, and the

Busbys, who are Loyalists but "not out of the top drawer." *Morning at Jalna* (1960), Mazo's last novel and second in the chronological sequence, reveals a strong correspondence between the Busbys and the Lundys:

> Elihu Busby had reared a large family. They were in some awe of him but considered no people their betters. They combined an ardent loyalty to the Queen with a look askance at English manners. They liked the Whiteoaks but were often affronted by what they felt were their lofty ways. They cherished an undying dislike of Americans and exaggerated the importance of the property they had left behind, two generations ago, in Pennsylvania.

In *Morning at Jalna*, the differences between the Whiteoaks and the Busbys are further articulated when the Whiteoaks are visited by the Sinclairs, courtly southern plantation owners, themselves exiles during the American Civil War. Whereas the Whiteoaks are sympathetic to the South, which they see as having traditions and roots in keeping with their own, the Busbys, while despising Americans, are active supporters of the North; one of Elihu's sons joins the Union army. Although the narrator's attitude towards the Sinclairs is best characterized as ambivalent (they are still Americans!), the Busbys are not presented in an especially favourable light. Indeed, Elihu's outspoken opposition to the South and slavery is regarded by the Whiteoaks as an indication of his extremism and inferior social status.

In *The Building of Jalna* (set in the early 1850s, a decade before *Morning at Jalna*), the British settlers who have arrived in the area after Busby — whose land has been granted to him because of his Loyalist sympathies — are antirepublican and exemplars of a rigid social hierarchy. David Vaughan, a retired Anglo-Indian colonel, and a confrère of Philip's, invites the Whiteoaks, who have been left property in Quebec, to remove to this part of Ontario, where "an agreeable settlement of *respectable* families is being formed," and where Captain Whiteoak and his "talented lady" will receive the welcome "that people of your consequence *merit*"; he tells Philip that his aim is to keep the settlement "purely British." "No Irish?"

asks Adeline. Captain Whiteoak's answer to his wife's inquiries about their new neighbours is unequivocal as to what confers respectability and consequence:

> A quite respectable and well-informed circle.... Their sincere hope is to keep it free of foreigners. They want to build up the population slowly but solidly out of sturdy British material.... [T]hese people from Eastern and Southern Europe would as soon as not stick a knife into your back.... I've lived a good many years in India and I've seen enough of treachery. Let's go slow and sure. Let's keep British.

Indeed, David Vaughan has invited Whiteoak into his circle because his blue-eyed, blond-haired friend can be trusted to exhibit the xenophobia that flourished in the Indian garrison town after which Philip's estate is to be named.

This time, Adeline's response to Philip's vow to keep the enclave British is to change the interrogative to a declarative — "*And* Irish" — unconsciously, one suspects, expressing Mazo's defensive social insecurity. The Courts, Adeline's Irish clan, in fact regard themselves as above the Whiteoaks, aristocrats distinguished by their patrician noses: Adeline is the granddaughter of a marquis. Thus, rather than identifying with the Busbys, Mazo turned to the Whiteoaks, who, in fact, elevated *their* social standing through an alliance with the Courts, idealized conceptions of her Irish ancestors, the "distinguished nobodies" of whom she wrote in her autobiography.

Mazo's romantic dissemination of the Loyalist myth conceals a crisis of identity inherent in the Upper Canadian social vision. As I have already noted, when the Loyalists — and we must remember that they were an extremely heterogeneous group — were expelled from the United States, they were forced to invent an identity. They responded by defining themselves through a passionate, if ambivalent, anti-Americanism and the belief that they were British. Veneration of the family, respect for authority and inherited power, resistance to American materialism through devotion to the land (qualities named by Fellows) — these were the defenses erected by the Loyalists against what David Bell has called "the paradox of being 'anti-American Yankee[s].'"

Bell has also observed that, from a psychological perspective, "Canada's relationship with the United States bears a number of pathological characteristics." Many of the Whiteoaks' attitudes, especially towards Americans, bear the imprint of their creator in that they exhibit what we might call delusions of grandeur. The biggest of these delusions is that this one-family garrison can resist and survive the changes that threaten its way of life after World War II.

In the novels following *The Building of Jalna*, Mazo's anti-Americanism, specifically her detestation of mass culture, materialism, and egalitarian ideals, becomes so pervasive that the Whiteoaks come to be less and less upholders of instinctive life and freedom and more and more prisoners of their obsession with order and continuity. Veneration of family translates into a blind surrender to Renny and Piers's hegemony, respect for authority and inherited power becomes a form of self-denial, and patriotism (attachment to the land) is confused with loyalism (attachment to the parent).[5]

Return to Jalna (1946) marks the beginning of this transformation. As the third-generation Whiteoak males find their way back to the ancestral home following the war, they retreat further and further into pastoral idealism. Renny epitomizes this response:

> He would stay at home and think easy and comfortable thoughts. He would forget the victimized world he had been living in for more than four years. He would forget the planes that swept like a flock of vultures; the palpitating entanglement of mechanism that ground that earth. He felt that he hated everything mechanical. He would like to walk on his two legs or ride a horse for the rest of his days. He felt that he would like to see the land ploughed, harrowed, sown with seed, by man's labour alone, as in the old days at Jalna. His ears were weary of the throbbing of engines.

Piers's return, preceding Renny's, symbolizes the intrusion of the mechanical world into the pastoral, implying not only the impossibility of returning to the old days at Jalna but also the sentimental underpinnings of the Loyalist myth. Mazo's archetypal farmer, tiller of the earth, the plowman of English tradition, Piers is now an amputee, his leg sacrificed on Old World soil. His legs were once "fine pillars" (*Whiteoak Brothers*); Piers now returns to the fields on an artificial limb. His scarred stump testifies to a symbolic castration: the steward of the land has been mutilated by twentieth-century technology and industrialism.

There is also a serpent in the Edenic garden to which Renny imagines he is returning — a retired businessman named Eugene Clapperton, who has purchased Vaughanlands, once a bastion of English colonial values. Clapperton's background identifies him with the forces of self-interest that were spawned south of the border, and he pollutes the pristine air of Jalna merely with his presence. His secretary, for example, secretly escorts Renny's daughter, Adeline, to see Paul Robeson in *Othello*; the play shifts him into hormonal overdrive, and, afterwards, he accosts young Adeline. Renny thrashes the secretary viciously, and then expresses to his wife the horror he feels at the thought of their daughter seeing Robeson — "a *negro* . . . !" — play Othello. He beats Adeline with his grandmother's ebony stick — one of old Adeline's favourite pastimes was flogging her grandsons — and the act serves to initiate the process of Papa's return to authority, completed when he accepts his daughter's invitation to lie in bed: "A sudden, dark possessiveness of fatherhood came over him. He would never willingly give her to any man. Not for years and years. He ran his hand along the outline of her body. She was breathing deeply." His resolution will resurface when Adeline finds a man she loves.

Earlier in the Jalna chronicles Maurice Vaughan reluctantly surrenders part of his patrimony by carving four building lots out of Vaughanlands; fortunately, Renny, through the agency of Sarah Court's fortune, is able to arrest the egalitarian tide by purchasing the land. Now, after the war, the threat is far greater, as Clapperton is planning to turn Vaughanlands into a model village of ticky-tacky bungalows (what Renny refers to as "Frankenstein's monster"). Although he at first succeeds in violating the sacred precincts of the Whiteoak manor, Clapperton eventually sacrifices his life to his avarice; in *Renny's Daughter*, Mazo's capitalist enters the manor at Vaughanlands after it has gone up in flames — he braves the conflagration of David Vaughan's imperial vision — in an attempt to rescue a silver tea service. His death effectively eliminates from the fictional realm the suburbanization that was taking place in Clarkson.

Significantly, the year of *Return to Jalna*'s publication saw not only the sale of Trail Cottage but also the Corporation of Windsor's expropriation of Vale House. That year, 1946, also marked Mazo's move from Windrush Hill to Forest Hill. Barbara Larson recalls that Mazo and Caroline were "a little upset that they had put themselves so far out because they found it very difficult to get into Toronto"; a record-breaking cold spell in 1943, shortages caused by the war, and the ill health of both Mazo and Caroline had aggravated this isolation. At the same time, in relocating to Russell Hill Road, at the heart of the residential garrison of Toronto's plutocracy, Mazo was confirming her position in the world.

After a writing hiatus of nearly two years, brought on by her ill health, worries about Caroline, and the move to Toronto, Mazo plunged into *Mary Wakefield*, which she set in the early 1890s. Recent commentators on the novel, published in 1949, have argued that this story of the second Philip Whiteoak's courtship of his children's governess (after whom the book is named) subverts the romance formula: Mary is involuntarily cast in the conventional role of governess/wife/mother, to which she succumbs after a period of spirited resistance. Certainly, the debate between Philip and Admiral Lacey suggests that Mazo was questioning other conventions, as well. Philip, complaining that the neighbourhood clings too tightly to British ways and that the Whiteoaks, Vaughans, and Laceys imported their own prejudices, is interrupted by the admiral: "Very well. Prejudices. Prejudice against making a fetish of material progress — against all the hurry-scurry after money that goes on in the big American cities. They wanted to lead contented peaceful lives and teach their children to fear God, honor the Queen, fight for her if necessary. In short, behave like gentlemen." Philip politely retorts that Canada cannot go on modelling itself after the Old Country forever, adding that his family, in its attempt to bring up its children to be just like English ones, can't hope to succeed. He shocks his listeners with the prediction that Canadians will eventually become "a good deal Americanized."

Written at a time when Mazo's own children were becoming thoroughly Canadianized, the passage does not strike the reader as a blanket endorsement of the admiral's view, nor does it suggest that Mazo regarded England's dying influence in unequivocal terms. Still, while Philip is clearly presented as a realist, as well as a budding nationalist, there's no mistaking the author's partisanship with the admiral in his hatred of American materialism and deep-felt loyalty to the monarchy.

Philip's concern with the threat posed by mammonism is carried much further in the remaining Whiteoak chronicles. In *Renny's Daughter*, Mazo, returning to the postwar period, lashes out at everything Clapperton represents via a heated exchange between the master of Jalna and her caricatured entrepreneur. Arguing that civilization is going down the tubes with the proliferation of shoddy goods and jerry-built houses, Old Redhead finds that in order to maintain his peace of mind he must now remain within his own gates, for the world outside is full of traffic and burgeoning subdivisions; all that is beautiful and holy is being consumed by overriding greed. Such aristocratic displays of temper are upsetting to Clapperton, his emotions being as limited as his imagination.

Whiteoak Brothers, set in 1923, finds Jalna poised between the golden days and the oncoming nightmare. Driving down the road along the lakeshore to Stead (Oakville), Piers, who ironically dreams of coming affluence, is blissfully unaware of the devastation about to take place: "The oaks and pines, in their primeval grandeur, beneath which moccasined Indians had passed to meet the first traders, stood in ignorance of the advancing axe, the coming bungalow, the filth of factory." The palatial houses that are about to appear on the shoreline where Piers's family has picnicked for three generations will signify the triumph of the forces of conspicuous consumption. They will cut the land off from the lake and the freedom it symbolizes. Yet the canker of American materialism has already spread through the Whiteoaks of Jalna, for Piers's brother Eden, beguiled by an unctuous American stockbroker, has enticed members of the family to invest in fraudulent mining shares. This broker, Kronk, a Sam Slick of the Roaring Twenties, knows exactly how to dupe the ingenuous Canadian, telling Eden what wise investors the Whiteoaks are, given that Americans are grabbing up all the shares. (Renny demonstrates the same faith in Yankee shrewdness in Mazo's next narrative, wavering about whether to purchase a racehorse until he is told that some Americans are interested in the colt.)

Variable Winds at Jalna (1954) resounds with authorial vituperation towards encroaching mass culture. As members of the family casually discuss modern psychology, Archer Whiteoak, Renny and Alayne's son, expresses his desire to own a television. His mother is shocked: " 'Television,' repeated Alayne, to whom the word conjured up visions of repulsive faces and still more repulsive sounds. 'Oh, surely not, Archer.' " Yet television does come to Jalna — in Alayne's absence — and the installation of the aerial represents a watershed in the house's history. The narrator wonders what Archer's forbears might have thought of this thing that looks like a lightning rod, concluding,

> [N]ever in their most delirious imaginings would they have pictured the fantastic things that were projected on to the screen in the library. Yet their descendant, Archer Whiteoak, watched the grotesque, the inane, the sometimes revolting pictures with no more than a flicker on his pale face. He listened to noises called music, which would have caused those same grandparents of his to clap their hands over their ears in horror, and never turned a hair.

Alayne, returning from New York, finds to her own horror her husband and son planted in front of the screen, on which glows the image of heaving, sweating, nearly naked wrestlers who resemble "prehistoric monsters in obscene conflict." Yet even she succumbs to the lure of the screen when she discovers an orchestra playing Mozart there.

It's ironic that the master of Jalna, who was so terribly upset that his wife had installed a radiator in the hall while *he* was absent during the war, should now be responsible for introducing a far more dangerous symbol of modernity into the house's sacred precincts. And it is even more ironic that, the second generation of Whiteoaks now deceased, the torch of civilized life should pass to Alayne Archer, whom J.G. Snell has identified as the one person at Jalna who symbolizes America. Mazo's presentation of Alayne in fact points to the ambivalence in Loyalist attitudes towards Americans, for on one hand Alayne is a sophisticated outsider in conflict with Jalna's natural, instinctive ways; yet on the other she demonstrates an intellectuality and urbanity that make the domain of the Whiteoaks appear provincial and even crude by comparison.

But then Alayne is a curious sort of American. The daughter and granddaughter of New England academics, she herself holds a degree from one of the Seven Sisters, though Uncle Nicholas Whiteoak proudly boasts of never having heard of Smith College. In the earlier chronicles, the Whiteoaks have been quick to make facile generalizations about Alayne — being American, she must be an heiress; being an American woman, she will attempt to break the spirit of her husband. They have never truly appreciated the special sort of American she is. In her youth, doing research for a history of the American Revolutionary War written by her father, she developed a great admiration for the Loyalists, "who had left their homes and journeyed northward into Canada to suffer cold and privation for the sake of an idea" (*Jalna*).

Mazo, in creating Alayne Archer, brought into the Whiteoak constellation a representative of American culture and prosperity who, though sympathetic to the Loyalist vision, is forever set apart from what Jalna symbolizes. Alayne's separateness is enforced through the author's usual strong differentiation of gender: Loyalist/British Canada is assigned the masculine principal; republican America is assigned the feminine. In *Variable Winds at Jalna*, the Virginia creeper that covers the house — the stalk of its rugged vine reminding Alayne of a man's hairy arm — comes to have anthropomorphic significance, for she imagines this symbol of Whiteoak masculinity laughing at her as it sends forth fresh tendrils.

Repeatedly affiliating the Whiteoaks with the archetypal Green Man of pagan religions, Mazo, in contrast, emphasizes the repressive side of Alayne's nature, and thus hints that the wild Green Man will be eliminated by the official culture. Although Alayne is represented as a civilizing influence, Mazo has manipulated the reader's response by investing her emissary from the Atlantic seaboard with national attributes of which she intends readers to be wary. Essential to the Loyalist vision is an emotional, indeed irrational, devotion to the family and to the land as the basic components of a separate order based on nature (see Fellows); the Whiteoaks embody this belief, and whenever Alayne opposes their masculinity she is also deconstructing a mythology.

FIGURE 17

The photograph Mazo sent the Harrises with her Christmas card in 1958. The golden retriever, named Tawny, belonged to René.

An ambivalence to American values even appears in one of Mazo's two books for children, *The Song of Lambert* (1955), in which a lamb with a melodious voice is seized from his pastoral setting by a wealthy American businessman from the city, Eugene Clapperton become Mr. van Grunt. The ailing van Grunt has been advised by his doctor to partake of an Antarctic expedition, but because he can only eat fresh meat, he acquires Lambert as provision. Ironically, Lambert becomes quite fond of the American businessman, while remaining ignorant of his intentions. When they reach the pole, they find that the Americans have already defaced it with a red neon sign. This bit of colour amidst the whiteness reminds Lambert of the organic world from which he has come, and he breaks into song. Van Grunt, awakened by the sweet music, joins the lamb in gambolling about in the moonlight, assuring Lambert: "You are the sweetest lamb I have ever known and I would rather die than harm you." Lambert returns home to his mother, twin sister, and the friendly mare who shares their pasture, assuring his dam, who once knew a pig named van Grunt, that *his* American millionaire is a gentleman.

If this tale — followed by *Bill and Coo* (1958), in which two pigeons sire a seraph — suggests that Mazo's writing had become saccharine, *Centenary at Jalna*, also published in 1958, presents a very different picture. Ostensibly a story of celebration, the last novel in the chronology actually offers the darkest view of the Whiteoak dynasty. Not only does the undercurrent of familial psychosis erupt in the fourth generation, but also Renny's patriarchal dominance and ancestor worship come to seem hostile to the very life for which he originally stood.

The novel was written at 3 Ava Crescent in Forest Hill. This was to be Mazo's last home, and its English vernacular architecture evoked for her the time she had spent in Britain. Yet *Centenary at Jalna* all but acknowledges the impossibility of replicating a vanishing world of English values in postwar Canada. It also presents the Loyalist dream turned nightmare. Even the preparations for Jalna's one-hundredth anniversary are debased by ubiquitous popular culture: when Renny has the old house tarted up for the occasion by having its outdoor woodwork painted an ivory colour, he compares the ancestral home to a glamorous blonde, to which Alayne, quoting from a radio soap advertisement, ironically rejoins, "It 'has that ivory look.'"

Also to mark the centenary, Piers's son Christian (another Whiteoak artist figure) paints portraits of his brother Philip and cousin Adeline, who are to marry. Their union, masterminded by their fathers, Piers and Renny, is to be the crowning glory of the centenary, for the betrothed cousins are the spitting images of Captain Philip Whiteoak and his wife, Adeline, whose original portraits are family totems. The young couple's physical beauty, the fruit of four generations of Whiteoak-Court breeding, masks the spiritual incompatibility at the core of their relationship. Adeline, whose Irish lover has run off with her illegitimate cousin Roma after Renny's heavy-handed interference in her affair of the heart, feels no love for her blue-eyed, blond-haired fiancé; when Renny envisions "Another Philip and Adeline," she reasons, "Life is different now, Daddy. There isn't the same *belief*." Philip, however, a gorgeous lunkhead who claims that mental strain puts him to sleep, hankers for the power over his strong-willed cousin that he believes will come to him through their intimacy. The hollow triumph of Renny and Piers's egotism, grounded in an obsessive devotion to a *"belief,"* constitutes a sordid final chapter to the history of a family that once balanced instinctive longing for freedom with the demands of tradition. If, as Douglas Daymond has said, this balance in a sense "embodied central ingredients of an entire culture" ("Whiteoak Chronicles"), the supplanting of personal freedom by tradition and order must be seen as the author's gloomy appraisal of the world from which she was about to depart.

Even more disturbing, however, is the presence in the novel of young Dennis Whiteoak, Finch's son by Sarah Court. A demonic sadist who has attempted to drown his baby cousin, Dennis systematically tortures the psyche of his new stepmother, Sylvia Fleming. The culmination of his vicious behaviour — Dennis "long[s] for violence" — occurs when he deliberately exhausts his father's pregnant wife as he romps with her in the snow; afterwards, when Sylvia has gone into labour, Dennis refuses to call the doctor, enjoying a sense of power as he hears her agonized screams. Sylvia's rolling, bloodshot eyes grotesquely fixed upon him, Dennis finally gives his dying stepmother the telephone number of the local veterinarian, then deliberately opens the door to the freezing outdoors, shouting "Go ahead! Have your monster! That's what it's going to be, you know — a monster — a monster. My father doesn't want it — I don't want it — it's yours." Thus speaks the only child of the character with whom Mazo "was one." In a speech she made at a banquet back in May of 1927, the prizewinning author of *Jalna* was reported as stating that "she had never finished a novel without looking back to the beginning, to the darkness she had had to pierce and in which she seemed to live with her characters" (Sandwell). Piercing the darkness in her penultimate novel, Mazo lived with her own monster.

Dennis, who has been shockingly neglected by Finch, drives his sensitive father to distraction through his mere presence. He may be seen as a disturbing gloss on the psychic life that Mazo, now a grandmother, experienced in her later years. A far cry from the cloyingly lovable children of *Beside a Norman Tower* and *The Very House*, this twisted Whiteoak of the fourth generation seems to embody the suggestion that the author, like the governess in James's *The Turn of the Screw*, had looked evil straight in the eye.

If only Mazo had stopped there. But her American publishers, eager to cash in on the earlier success of *Gone With the Wind*, had improvidently suggested she write a novel set during the period of the American Civil War, and *Morning at Jalna* resulted. With its references to slave children as "pickaninnies" and its stereotypical representation of the shifty Native half-breed, it is an ignominious swan song for an author whose earlier narratives celebrated the life of which she now seemed so afraid. Yet even here there are wonderful moments, none so fine as the fourteenth chapter, when the second-generation Whiteoaks run away on a sailboat, venturing out on the lake in quest of freedom. Their adventure links them to the adventuring Curzon boys; both sets of siblings belong to the world of the Play. Mazo had travelled full circle.

In 1958, she and Caroline made their final visit to England, with Macmillan marking the occasion by fitting up the St. Martin's House office as a replica of Jalna. Yet the London media were cruelly cynical at the press conference held upon her arrival (Givner); the critical tide had long since turned against her for having churned out one Whiteoak novel after another at the prompting of her publishers. Although Mazo was sustained by the devotion of her loyal readers, to whom she dedicated much of her time in correspondence, she felt betrayed and neglected by those closest to her.

Mazo had, for example, fired off a letter to Edward Weeks in 1956 in which she expressed these feelings in the context of his rejection of her short story "The Father," where strong undercurrents of father-daughter incest were again in evidence:

> As to The Father, you say you do not see him as you believe I saw him in my mind. He seems to you "a good deal of a nonenity" [sic]. I saw him, as it were, not a violent man but rather a peaceful one who had been flattened out by twenty years in prison. I did not intend this picture of him to be dramatic or tragic. Neither did I intend his longing for his daughter to "descend into bathos." That word, I think, has never before been used about my writing. In any case I have swallowed the rather unpalatable pill that I am no longer capable of writing anything you want for the pages of The Atlantic. Therefore I shall not again offer you anything.

The letter's tone is reminiscent of that of a letter Mazo had written to Weeks much earlier, in 1934, in which she assailed him for Macmillan of Canada's taking all the credit for commissioning a leather-bound copy of *The Master of Jalna*, which she had autographed and personally presented to Queen Mary at the request of Sir Walter R. Lawrence. This incident relates to a final irony in the life of a Loyalist.

Reading in Joan Givner's biography that, according to a Montreal journalist in the early 1950s, Queen Elizabeth II's interest in her future dominion had been formed by reading the Jalna books, I wrote to Her Majesty not only about this matter but also the whereabouts of the autographed copy of *The Master of Jalna*. I received from Buckingham Palace a reply, dated 4 August 1994: the queen commands her secretary to inform me that she does not remember reading the Jalna books, and that there is no trace in the Royal Library of the signed copy of *The Master of Jalna* said to have been given to Queen Mary.

Mazo's 1954 Christmas card to Annie Sayers included a note telling her, "My play, *Whiteoaks*, was performed in Ottawa in the presence of the Queen Mother, and I had the honour of being presented to her." When Mazo de la Roche died in Forest Hill on 12 July 1961, with Caroline Clement at her side, she left behind memories of Queen Mary's earlier visits to productions of *Whiteoaks*, and of beautiful gardens she had known in all the lovely old houses in which she and Caroline had spent their halcyon days in the 1930s. Perhaps there is a lesson to the Loyalist here. To Mazo, and to the Whiteoaks, patriotism and loyalism were inseparable — attachment to the soil of Canada and attachment to the parent in England were one and the same. Had this not been so, her writing might not have suffered the fate that it did during the days of rising Canadian nationalism.

But if Mazo has been largely forgotten in Canada and England, her devotion to her French ancestry has been rewarded. In 1994, millions of viewers in the French-speaking world tuned in their televisions to *Jalna*, the sixteen-million-dollar series produced by the France 2 network, to follow the lives of a Gallicized Whiteoak family. *Gammon!*

Hands

Hands (especially those of artists) had a special significance for Mazo, and she uses them throughout her work both as indications of character and as instruments of creativity and sexuality. It seems likely that she made the successful artist of the Whiteoak family a pianist in part because a pianist's instrument of expression is the hands. And she wished to include a photograph of her own hands in her autobiography. (Givner)

Always can I remember her hands, long, white and extraordinarily supple. They were inherited by my father, the one characteristic he had from her. I do not think these hands of Grandmama's had ever been used for anything more strenuous than needlework. They lay, long and white, on the arms of her chair. Sometimes she would raise them from the wrist and gently let them fall again, while she uttered a resigned "heigh-ho." (*Ringing*)

In that year I always seemed to have a pencil in my hand, always making sketches. Once when I went to sit with Grandpa I took my drawing block. He was asleep and his hands were loosely clasped on the counterpane. I thought how beautiful they looked and I made a drawing of them, as he slept.... Later on I felt great shame that I should have made a drawing of a dying man's hands, while he lay there helpless. It seemed somehow disloyal, but always there was in me that urge to create. I tore the drawing into small pieces. (*Ringing*)

Let me describe us. First there was my mother — five foot three of nervous sensibility and indomitable spirit.... Her hands and feet were beautiful. W.O. Forsyth, who was a musician and teacher of note, gave her piano lessons when she was young. He told me that, all through the lesson, he could not forget her lovely hands. I think she had little or no talent for music. (*Ringing*)

Pierre came from New York to see me and to talk, but though he was there in the flesh — his thick black hair the same; his amber eyes looking contemplatively into mine; his beautiful hands making just a few, very expressive gestures — he still seemed far away ... (*Ringing*)

No longer did my father take his walks. When he rose in mid-morning he sat in a chair facing the faded mirror that gave him back his melancholy reflection. Now it might be seen that he had given up all hope.
  Looking at him one day, sitting there, unseen by him, I remembered how, in strange foreboding, I had more than once, joyful in his homecoming, thought: "How many more times shall we, united, embrace? ..."
  Now in midsummer he died.... Caroline, thinking only of others, attended to the things that must be done. Her courage never failed us. It was she who carried the lilies my mother had gathered, and laid them near his folded hands. (*Ringing*)

Something made me hold out my hand ... a beautiful Irish hand, the one part of myself of which I am vain. (*Thunder*)

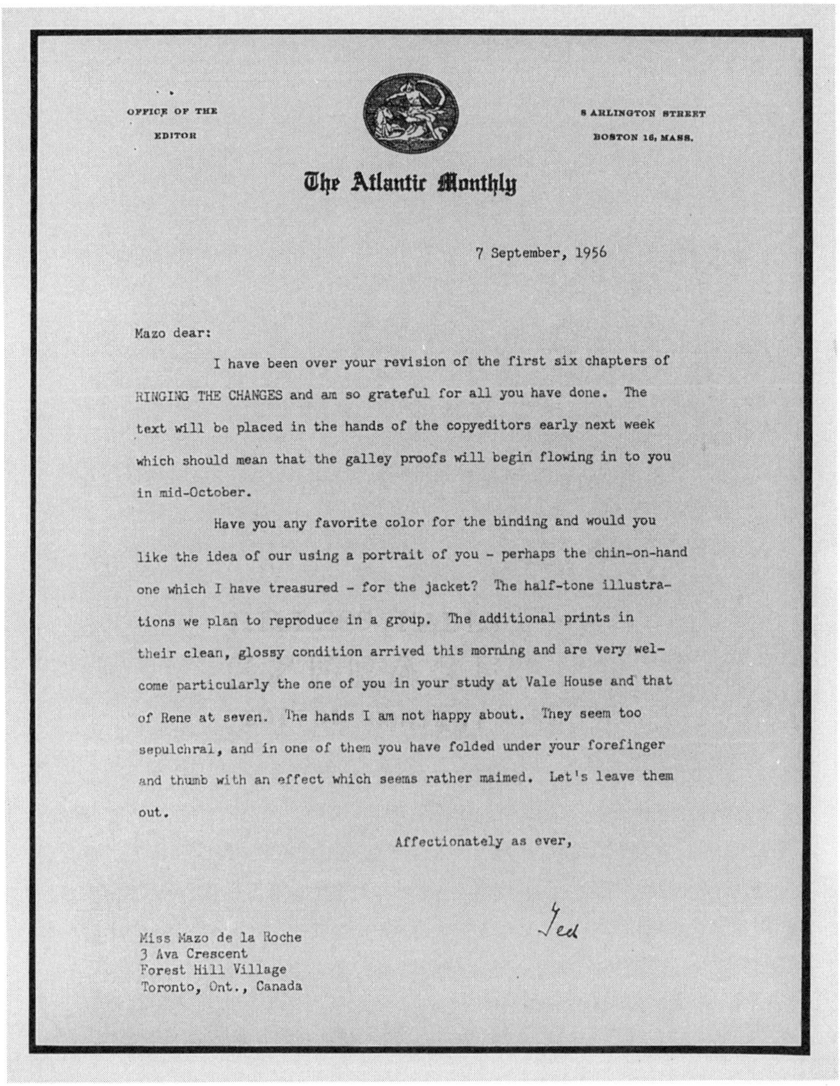

OFFICE OF THE EDITOR

The Atlantic Monthly

8 ARLINGTON STREET
BOSTON 16, MASS.

7 September, 1956

Mazo dear:

    I have been over your revision of the first six chapters of RINGING THE CHANGES and am so grateful for all you have done. The text will be placed in the hands of the copyeditors early next week which should mean that the galley proofs will begin flowing in to you in mid-October.

    Have you any favorite color for the binding and would you like the idea of our using a portrait of you - perhaps the chin-on-hand one which I have treasured - for the jacket? The half-tone illustrations we plan to reproduce in a group. The additional prints in their clean, glossy condition arrived this morning and are very welcome particularly the one of you in your study at Vale House and that of Rene at seven. The hands I am not happy about. They seem too sepulchral, and in one of them you have folded under your forefinger and thumb with an effect which seems rather maimed. Let's leave them out.

                      Affectionately as ever,

                                            Ted

Miss Mazo de la Roche
3 Ava Crescent
Forest Hill Village
Toronto, Ont., Canada

FIGURE 18

Edward Weeks's letter of 7 September 1956 rejecting Mazo's plan to have a photograph of her hands in *Ringing the Changes*.

```
                                    MACMILLAN & CO., LTD.
TELEGRAMS:"PUBLISH LESQUARE LONDON"
    CABLES:"PUBLISH LONDON"         ST. MARTIN'S STREET,
  TELEPHONE: WHITEHALL 8831
  CODE - 5TH AND 6TH EDITIONS A.B.C. LONDON, W.C.2.
   PLEASE QUOTE   LD/BP

                                         12th September, 1956.

      Miss Mazo de la Roche,
      3 Ava Crescent,
      Forest Hill Village,
      Toronto,
      Ontario,
      Canada.

           My dear Mazo,

                Thank you for your letter of August 31st which came in
           while I was away from the office on a short visit to a hos-
           pital.  I have now returned perfectly fit.

                Thank you for the additional photographs for RINGING THE
           CHANGES.  Some of these will be most useful.  The one of the
           mothers of you and Caroline is particularly interesting, and it
           is nice to have the picture of Vale House.

                We have gone very carefully into all these, and have made
           up a list, which I attach for you to see.  These are the
           pictures which we would like to use, and the order given is
           that which we propose to follow, unless you have other views.

                I feel on the whole that the photograph of your hands
           which while extremely interesting to anyone who knows you,
           would not be of sufficient interest to the many readers we hope
           to find for this book, and while the pictures of Rene and Esme,
           besides being very attractive, are essential to the story, I do
           not think the one of Rene's Alixe can be used; it is too far
           removed from the reader's interest in your life.

                I hope you will like the selection we have made and the
           order in which we have placed them, but do not hesitate if you
           would like this altered in any way.

                With love to you both,

                                         Yours ever,

                                         Rache
      Enc.                                           Lovat Dickson
```

FIGURE 19

Letter dated 12 September 1956 in which Lovat Dickson, Mazo's editor at Macmillan, concurs with Weeks (see fig. 18).

"Mazo de la Roche and The Whiteoaks of Jalna": The Author's Interview with Timothy Findley

Mr. Findley, you have stated that it's your firm belief that Mazo de la Roche used the Sibbalds and their estate on the shores of Lake Simcoe as her model for the Whiteoaks and Jalna. Would you be referring to Eildon Hall or The Briars, and why do you see the Sibbalds of Sutton rather than the Harrises of Clarkson in this role?

This is purely a personal interpretation, but I've always thought the Harrises of Clarkson are a red herring. Everything has been far too deliberate about setting them in place. Such an effort was made to set them in place so precisely. If it were a mystery novel, the clue would lie in some mismanaged "fact" about the Harris family. The truth is always haphazard. The Harris story is simply too precise. The Sibbalds, on the other hand, represent a wonderful coincidence.

The lake, for instance, is all that's ever mentioned in the books: it's never called "Lake Ontario"; the lake could well be Lake Simcoe. Why not? If you have read the geography of the Jalna books — as I had to in order to do the television series — you can go to Jackson's Point and Sibbald Point and practically track every step taken from the 1800s to 1954 — including all the steps down to the rectory, the church, and the little bower gate that passes between them — the churchyard and the position of all the family houses. It's all there. It's all on Hedge Road at Jackson's Point, on the south side of Lake Simcoe. Not only that, if you read even the most brief commentary on the history of the Sibbald family — which is given, for instance, on placards (that used to be, at any rate), in Sibbald Park — it tells how the Sibbalds were a matriarchal family, established in Canada when they moved from a colonial outpost in India — British military. It is, simply, Granny Whiteoak and her family. *Please!* Can people read?

Then you have the undeniable evidence of Mazo de la Roche and Caroline Clement both being buried in that little Anglican churchyard at Sibbald Point. Not as if Clarkson had no graveyards. . . . On the other hand, the Clarkson house is undeniably dull — it isn't even pretty! Whereas Eildon Hall is a glorious monument to British aristocratic architecture in a lovely Anglified setting.

I have never talked to any of the present members of the Sibbald family about this, but my own sense is that at some point, Mazo may well have requested — and received — permission from the Sibbalds of her day to use their history in her novels. There is nothing other than the basic family history — the circumstances — to suggest this connection. So far as I know, there are no Renny's lurking in Sibbald bushes. I don't know how the surviving Sibbalds might feel about it. There are aspects of the Whiteoak family that are not terrific. That's another story. Most of what is unpleasant comes, I think, from Mazo herself — and *that* is another story, too.

Not long ago I heard that you joked on [CBC Radio's] Morningside about your ancestry being linked illegitimately — or something to that effect — to Mazo de la Roche. What was that all about?

My joke about Mazo and Stephen Butler Leacock was first given as a speech at a Leacock Seminar at the University of Ottawa in 1985, then published in the proceedings of that seminar [see appendix] — and finally broadcast as part of a CBC *Morningside* tribute to Stephen Leacock in 1994. It had to do with the fact that Mazo de la Roche and Stephen Leacock are both buried in the Anglican cemetery at Sibbald Point, just a couple of hundred yards down the road from where my grandfather, Thomas Findley, had a summer cottage. (He grew up in Sutton West, and became president of Massey Harris.) Also, I had adapted the Jalna books for television, as well as having played Peter Pupkin in a CBC Television series based on Leacock's *Sunshine Sketches of a Little Town*. I used all these clues — plus a few literary details from my own work — to "prove" that I was, in fact, the descendant not of Thomas Findley, but of a hitherto undiscovered liaison between Mazo de la Roche and Stephen Butler Leacock. It was a joke. On the other hand . . . my nose — my ears — my lisp . . . some would say an uncanny resemblance . . .

When I asked you for this interview you replied that while the CBC Jalna series broadcast in 1972 offers few happy memories, you would not mind talking about the project. How did you come to be involved in The Whiteoaks of Jalna, *and what were the circumstances surrounding the writing of the scripts for the episodes?*

I was brought into the project, I suspect, because they were looking for writers who had a concept and sense of "period" — and I had demonstrated that I did have some idea of what "period writing" was about. I think partly it must have been the suggestion of Alice Sinclair, the series script editor, who had a sympathetic sense of what my work was about.

Unfortunately, top to bottom, the experience was not a happy one. (The actors, I hasten to add, were a joy to work with.) But probably the only "nice" person who worked on that whole series — in any executive position — was the editor just mentioned, Alice Sinclair. Ms. Sinclair, I regret, is now dead. She was wonderful — a woman I had known all my professional life. When I first encountered her in the mid- to late 1940s, I was a very young actor and she was still married to Lister Sinclair, the writer-broadcaster.

Alice was also the *Jalna* unit's liaison with Caroline Clement. It was poor Alice who had to do all that to-ing and fro-ing and settling of Caroline's mind at ease over how the series was being done. Caroline was bedridden and dying and totally against the CBC decision to bring part of every episode into the present — the present then being the early 1970s. And Alice was wonderful. She soothed Caroline and saved *Jalna*. Some would say *"saved Jalna,* when the 1970s were made part of it?" Forgetting, of course, that what Caroline wanted to protect was not *Jalna*, but Mazo — and Mazo, she saved. With Alice Sinclair's delicate, humorous, and wonderful tact.

Whose decision was it to bring the series forward in time, beyond Centenary at Jalna?

The head of TV drama then, at the CBC, was Fletcher Markle — and the producer (and director of some of the episodes) was John Trent. My companion, Bill Whitehead, who survived all my traumas over this series, once remarked that Trent was a "professional son-of-a-bitch" working in a situation that needed a professional son-of-a-bitch or the project could not have been brought to fruition. And

John — who is, alas, also dead now — played the role of the son-of-a-bitch very well. I don't know whether it was his idea, or Fletcher's, to bring part of the series into the present. (Bill Whitehead maintains he remembers it was Fletcher, who was doing the series because of the great success of the British series, *The Forsyte Saga* — but Fletcher Markle did not want to be accused of merely copying the Brits, and so he landed on this "modern" twist.)

This is, I think, a good moment to pause and reflect on the death of John Trent. What we all have to do — all of us who were involved in the *Jalna* series, is give thanks — a moment's silence — in John's behalf. Forget, here, about television/movies — and ambition. We all have that. Never to be forgotten, from my point of view, is the moment of John's death. A man I admired, but with whom I had argued — disagreed with — disapproved of — had died — *been killed*. How? Well, he died for others. Given five seconds of choice on a bad road, he drove straight into an oncoming car and saved, thereby, the passengers of a yellow school bus. One death — John's. The rest — *everyone* — lived. I knew this man. His death does not and did not surprise me. What did surprise me was the power of his absence. He was — uniquely — wonderful.

Now — the rest. John certainly went along with the idea — to relate all of Mazo's stories to "now" — the 1970s and drug-ridden youth, et cetera. It was, of course, hogwash. Pure, unadulterated hogwash. It was money — buying money. The original stories had already come about as far as the end of Mazo's life in the 1950s. So — why would you bring them any further forward? The stories were perfectly ended in the 1950s, which was already a conservative period, matching the tenor of her books. Who needed the 1970s?

Anyway, the arguments, the ultimate critical reception — maybe I should say, critical "rejection" — it was all totally unpleasant. Endless quarrels about what should be in the scripts, how to bring them up to date . . .

Vile things happened. Markle could be an absolute bastard. At one point, early on, I tried to bring an agent into our negotiations. Fletcher rose from behind his desk, and fumed: "if you mention the word *agent* once more in this office, you will be fired!" No kidding. He went scarlet in the face. "Take it or leave it" was all there was.

Then we had strikes. We were only about two weeks into filming, and Kate Reid and Milly Hall and all the people who had to get into old-age makeup at five or six every morning got on the set in these ghastly latex masks — and then would be told to *stand by* while someone *fixed a light — adjusted a ladder — reset a chair* — and not one foot of film would be shot because the technical unions were working to rule. It was appalling. For the actors — for all the artists. It was a nightmare from start to finish.

Why did I do it? Well — a cheap question — my own — gets a cheap answer: *I wanted the experience. I wanted the money.*

I was not having a good time as a novelist, that work was not being received well — this was just halfway through the almost ten years that separated my first two books from *The Wars*. And so, in order to keep the *Jalna* job, I concurred with this inane decision. I became part of a pattern that should not have been established in the first place.

I think one of the many things that did not get well handled was this: we had just passed through the 1960s; the Vietnam War and Nixon were still with us; Watergate had just begun to happen. Our own country was in trouble — the bad things happening in Quebec in the 1970s — and the world at large was not in a terrific state. Basically because, there had been too much right-wing politicking and all the 1960s assassinations — Kennedy — Kennedy — King — and the killings at Kent State. The history of the whole times was appalling. Appalling — and, *conservative*-ridden. And if you want to meet a conservative, you've got one in Mazo de la Roche.

So, here we had this God-given gift of however many books there were of this family saga and there's just been this huge success with *The Forsyte Saga* — "we can make a killing for Canada! We can sell it abroad! There's a commercial market for this! It will make all our names!"

And so forth and so forth. Everyone forgetting that what they were buying into was an ultraconservative vision of paradise. That, alas, is what Mazo was about. *Class. Caste. Place. I am waiting for you to salute me.* What she wrote was Chekhov without the regret — without the compassion — without social conscience.

On.

But it was difficult to approach the business of producing this saga in the state of mind we were in — and by *we* I mean Fletcher Markle and John Trent and Alice Sinclair and Timothy Findley. We were on the left, politically, and not too happy with the characters we were being given to play with — especially at that point in history. We wanted to inject a sense of the destructive consequences when people's lives are politically self-centred. Certainly, we wanted to draw everything out of them that Mazo had put there — but instead of moving the plot lines, as she did, to benefit the *conservative* ideals of the Christian tradition — family and so on — we wanted to bring them up to date and keep them current with the political feeling of that time. This proved — why am I laughing? — to be extremely difficult. On the other hand, where you can win in this situation is where you have characters such as Adeline Whiteoak — "Granny." She was herself — no other — a wonderful feisty warrior against whatever presented itself as standing in her path. Also, the character of Renny, her grandson, who was Rhett Butler, Angel Clare, and Dracula, all in one.

So you had some good strong characteristics to deal with, but the setting — the rural manor — was the traditional setting of the conservative novel. Let's all go down to the church, he said. Let's all fall on our knees and pray. Family values — while you lust after your cousin. And that was very difficult to achieve in the early 1970s when God-fearing morality was the everyday norm. The instinct to be sceptical of men who held up their fingers in the victory sign, saying: "I am not a crook," was thwarted by those values.

Had you already read all or most of the Jalna novels when you were asked to script the series, and had you read Ringing the Changes *and the plays?*

I had not read any of the plays and I still haven't. I had read *Ringing the Changes* — and I reserve comment. I never did read *all* the Jalna novels. But I did read the novels that were involved in the basic plotlines of episodes I was working with. This is where Alice Sinclair was a great help because she read virtually everything and provided synopses and we had marvellous conversations about what the characters and storylines were about.

One thing not to forget — there had been a superb radio adaptation of *Jalna* in the 1940s, and I played the young Finch and had terrific scenes with Granny Whiteoak, who was played by that wonderful woman, Jane Mallett. You want privilege? You had it, working with Jane. So that was my introduction to the Jalna books. And I had seen Mazo, once, on the street in Toronto. And this had some importance; Mazo was an icon.

My mother and I were walking on Bloor Street, near where the Ladies' Club used to be, and a big black car with a chauffeur stopped and Mazo was let out and she looked something like the character actress in the movies — Edna May Oliver — tall, angular, not pretty. But she had presence — she had style and absolute graces. My mother said to me — I was still a child — "Look, and remember this. That is Mazo de la Roche!" As though one were seeing God. This fed, of course, into my relationship with the Jalna novels. And the Whiteoaks.

To move from Bloor Street to the countryside, it seems to me that Mazo's concern — particularly in the postwar Jalna novels — with the destruction of the southern Ontario landscape leads directly into your own preoccupation with our being at war with nature. When you worked on the television series did this relation between your early novels and hers influence your writing?

There is some relationship between her written concerns and mine. But what has to be confronted here is: what did Mazo mean when she wrote about the destruction of southern Ontario's countryside and what did I mean when I wrote about it? I think I was talking about a different kind of destruction. My concerns were wholly with the destruction of nature, whereas Mazo's concern with the landscape was with "landscape" that had been conceived as something cultivated in the aristocratic British fashion.

There's nothing wrong with that, I hasten to add. It's just that the basis of Mazo's concern seems to have to do with land holdings and the uses of land by families who, like the Whiteoaks, had huge estates and basically ran them as they would in England. Tenants, cottagers, a central hall or manor — villages clustered around churches, everything dedicated to the aristocratic uses of nature. Whereas I wasn't writing about that at all, even though I had some affection for the memory of what had come out of the aristocratic uses of the landscape. I should explain: when you go to Britain now, you see the worst of what is happening (which, of course, has long ago happened here in Canada) and this is the horror of the mega-use — the corporate use — of the landscape. I have always been opposed to this — to Agrabiz. And I think Mazo de la Roche would have been opposed to it, too. In fact, I'm certain if she had lived long enough to see the corporate encroachment, she would have screamed bloody murder. The corporate uses of the land are as Genghis Khan is to the best of princes. In that sense, the aristocratic uses of the land — barring their relationship to the people who work on the land — were and are the saving grace: the cultivation, the protection, the sense that people still revered a landscape.

I think of the land in France, for example, that's been cultivated for what? Fifteen hundred years? And it is still producing. Yet we have land in Canada — out west and in Ontario — that was first cultivated only a *hundred* years ago — much of which is now stone dead. STONE DEAD. That is what Mazo was opposed to — and there we meet.

When you were interviewed by June Callwood for her television programme National Treasures, *you spoke of your home, Stone Orchard, as a "place of life," giving back "the sense of the living, and of life itself." This would be a fair description, I think, of the fictional Jalna. Do you think that Jalna still speaks to us in this respect?*

Stone Orchard, where I live, and Jalna do have something in common, but what they don't share is why they were brought into being. There is always the impetus to make something better than what exists — to use what one knows of the best of the civilizing influences of education, knowledge, and concern, to help the land and its people and its beasts survive. But most of what Jalna was about was the aristocratic ideal of colonialism. The land was colonized — not peopled. At the same time, there was an attempt to preserve a pastoral ideal — a British ideal that did not transplant well. Mazo's way of fitting her people into that ideal — in terms of class relationships — was to allocate roles based on British traditions that were already passé in the United Kingdom when she gave them their Canadian face. Her characters are classic examples of the phrase "more British than the British." Whereas where and how we live has to do with everyone making something together — not the "manor house" ideal.

I think the Jalna books do still pertain. But their pertinence is tied to Mazo's original view of the Whiteoak family, not what became of them as she enlarged their story. In time, the books frittered away into mere romances, but the early ones were tough and clearheaded. All literature, in its way, is about survival, and that's what Mazo's early Jalna books are about. That's why they do retain pertinence.

Have you ever thought of the Winslows of [your] The Last of the Crazy People *as being the dark side of the Whiteoaks?*

I must admit that this question makes me laugh. Not at the questioner, but simply at the notion that there's a light side to the Whiteoaks! I mean, particularly with the later novels. If you want monsters, just look at the children! That's one of the things Mazo was brilliant about — her portrayal of devil-driven children. As far as any relationship between the Winslows and the Whiteoaks — I would put them all in one unhappy barrel. I think they're all cut from the same dreadful pinstripe. I cannot begin to imagine their not knowing each other. They probably met for lunch once a week.

To move on to your third novel, did working on The Whiteoaks of Jalna *in any way affect your writing of* The Wars?

The writing of the *Jalna* TV series didn't affect my writing of my novel, *The Wars*, but I know that *The Wars* was in the back of my mind in the early 1970s. This certainly affected how I approached the World War I episodes of the *Jalna* series. And certainly, since that war had been lying dormant in my mind since childhood — it was my parents' war, and particularly my Uncle Tif's war — it may have been my having to do those episodes that pushed a novel about the war to the surface. All I brought to *Jalna* was my sense of what that war had been about — as expressed, later, in *The Wars*. But neither had any direct effect on the other. It was simply that the person writing each of them had a background and an inner transcript rich in the voices of that war.

I must say here — and it struck me then — that the best of what John Trent was about was in the directing of those war episodes. He did a beautiful job of anything that had to do with that period. I will never forget the thrill of seeing that particular period come to life under his hand. John could play the son-of-a-bitch, but he was also an artist. He loved his work with actors and with cameras, and it shows best in those segments.

If I may return to your interview with June Callwood, in it you stated that where we are has a spiritual quality, that "everything is holy." You went on to speak of the body as a "biological entity born into a biological world," and not *born into the sidewalks. One of the reasons I'm writing this biography is to argue that Mazo de la Roche's fictions are about being fully alive or, to use your words, "totally connected" to the physical world. Her creation of Jalna and Gran Whiteoak testifies to this spiritual awareness, yet at the same time I feel there's something missing from her vision, perhaps related to her colonialism or — and I hope this isn't presumptuous given how she guarded her privacy — to the sadness that comes of unresolved conflicts of sexual identity, and therefore of the spirit. Can you help me out here?*

Yes, we were never meant to be born into a world of sidewalks. One thing we're all at war with is what the sidewalks do to us. They keep us from our biological birthplace. Mankind seems determined to deny that it inhabits the earth. Most of what mankind erects — cities and highways, et cetera — is a denial of the earth beneath our feet. Mazo was at war with that concept. So am I.

About colonialism — I come at least two generations after Mazo de la Roche — and yet the attitudes she knew as a child persisted into my time. We were brought up to believe that we had nothing to offer unless we offered it wearing white gloves and standing at attention. How dare we even think that we had anything original to say. That's what colonialism is about: *asking permission to exist.* Granny Adeline Whiteoak never asked anyone for permission to exist. This was a triumph. But — alas — over time, Mazo gave in. She became the *colonial's colonial* of literature. She went to England and lived in a manor house — as though to the manor born. She became a purveyor of colonialism, one of the Raj. It was odd — and I think sort of pathetic. But it made her happy.

About her sexual orientation: I've always felt a great deal of sadness on her behalf. She lived in a time when it simply wasn't countenanced. I don't know — who does? — to what extent her life and Caroline's were driven by lesbian sexuality, but they were definitely driven into one another's company by a profound sense of absolute love, person to person. That both of them happened to be women, in their time, created a kind of patina that allowed it to be acceptable, as long as one thought of them as *two ladies sharing life's storms because each had suffered the misfortune not to have been discovered by the right man.* What a bunch of claptrap! And what a bunch of claptrap they all had to suffer! Also — if they had been two *men*, they would have been ostracized. And of course it made tetchy, mean-spirited people of them, in a way. When society won't allow you to be who you are — you punish it. And Mazo punished her society by putting herself at one remove from it. But a noble aspect of their lives remains — namely, their total commitment, one human being to another.

Mazo, more than Caroline, decided that there should be children — and this was a ghastly mistake. A boy and a girl were adopted, and as I've said, if you want a portrait of children who were problematical, all you have to do is read the last novels. Big mistake, bringing children into a situation that really had only to do with two women and love, not with two women and a love of children. It was a mistake put upon her by her society. It was made to seem that if she was going to be Mazo de la Roche and have all that wealth and success and place — then one must fulfil one's duty and become a parent. Well, sorry, that won't necessarily work — and it sure didn't work for them.

Her vision is limited by the fact that she herself was limited by her doubts. Not fear. She was fearless. She was limited by the expectations of her society. "Ah, you've written a book, have you. Do give us another just like it!" They sucked her in, the way they had sucked in Lucy Maud Montgomery. *Anne and Emily forever!* and — *Jalna forever, too!* It was like a cancer, and it grew on Mazo like a cancer and it ate her alive.

Amen. Perhaps one of the reasons that critics in this country have been so unkind to Mazo de la Roche is that, while she examined the social history of southern Ontario to a greater degree than any other writer of her time, she never mentioned Toronto, never identified her locales by their actual names. So let's forget Can-lit and look at Mazo in relation to the larger tradition. What do you think is her place in that tradition?

Her reputation is secure. She put a particular world on the map of literature — a place that had never been on the literary map before. She was hugely successful in Europe, Britain, and the States — as well as Canada. The books gave an immensely popular concept of place and family at a time, in the 1920s, place and family were in jeopardy. Mazo's creation of Jalna and the Whiteoaks gave people a sense of confidence — the assurance that tie lines, even when cut, can be reconnected and can endure.

The way to discover if someone has a place in a body of literature is to remove them. And if you take Mazo de la Roche out of the body of literature, the body of literature suffers.

Thank you very much.

★ ★ ★

St. George's (Sibbald Memorial) Church, 3 September 1994: the congregation joins the organ in Beethoven's *Song of Joy*. It is a glorious, sun-drenched Sunday morning on the long weekend that sounds the death knell for summer holidays.

Peering as unobtrusively as possible into the vestibule, I find the memorial window dedicated "in abiding memory" to Mazo de la Roche. Fashioned in South Wales, it depicts St. Francis surrounded by birds, animals, and vegetation, the world that is the basis of all those fanciful Mazoian tropes. At the bottom is inscribed Coleridge's "He prayeth best who loveth best / all things both great and small."

There was no room left for a stained-glass window in the sanctuary, so Caroline and family had to settle for this tiny porch: to view the window properly one has to climb several of the narrow winding steps opposite it. Still, as I read in a guidebook I have taken from a rack that has been unceremoniously hung between the two panels of the window, Mazo's monument is "probably the tallest" in the churchyard.

I deposit two loonies for the booklet and wander past Stephen Leacock's gravestone, which is sheltered by a weeping mountain ash whose fruit contrasts brilliantly with the deep-blue sky. A Camper-

FIGURE 20

The Mazo de la Roche memorial window,
St. George's Church, Sibbald Point.

down elm used to stand here, but I've come too late to see it. I've also come too late to meet several people who knew Mazo; I discover that they'd died only a year or two ago.

Mazo, Caroline, and René's resting places directly overlook the lake, and searching for Orillia in the haze on the opposite shore, I remember Mazo's claim that while her life was a great struggle against ill health, she regained her strength summering at Lake Simcoe, a "friendlier" lake than Ontario. This is one of the most picturesque — and spiritually charged — settings for a graveyard in the entire country, I should think.

Her headstone is quintessential. Its Celtic cross signifies not only Mazo's Bryan and Roche ancestry — "the blood," Caroline Clement contended, "that ran in her veins" — but also, with its engraved flora and fauna, reminds us of the Gauls' adoration of the oak, and their worship of various animals. Its shaft bears a handsomely carved circle containing an apocryphal family motto: "MON DIEU EST MA ROCHE." Its base, like the memorial window, gives the wrong date of birth, 1888 — even today, the church guide lists Mazo's birthplace as Toronto. It is engraved, "DEATH INTERRUPTS ALL THAT IS MORTAL." As though to counter the weightiness of this pronouncement, however, there is a phoenix rising within the circle on the shaft: the bird is Mazo's totem; it makes me think of her staging another comeback.

The family plot is also rich in signification. Inlaid in the ground are two stones, one reading "BELOVED DAUGHTER OF WILLIAM RICHMOND AND ALBERTA DE LA ROCHE," the other engraved with the de la Roche patronymic that her parents never used. Caroline's monument assigns her the same year of birth as her cousin, its base testifying "HAND IN HAND WE KEPT THE FAITH." Though right next to Mazo's, it is, for the moment, kept in shadow by the branches of a large tree. Mazo's is in full light. Symbolism here, too.

Returning my gaze to the azure sweep of water, I suddenly feel a premonition of winter. In a few months, a cold wind will blow off the now-tranquil lake; drifts of snow will cover the icy surface of the vital water and bury the inscriptions at the foot of the markers. St. George's is shut up in winter, cutting the dead off from the rest of the world.

Eildon Hall, the great Sibbald matriarch's residence, is beyond the gates of the parking lot. Here my premonitions are confirmed — the old house, already boarded up for the winter, vacantly surveys the lonely expanse of water beyond. The first time I saw Benares, she, too, was boarded up. The same with Rochedale, now Sovereign House, on the shore of Lake Ontario. Like the Mazo de la Roche novels that gather dust on library bookshelves, these proud houses, closed to the world, appeared to be waiting.

I hold my breath.

"*This is what you have.*"

APPENDIX

RIDING OFF IN ALL DIRECTIONS
A Few Wild Words in Search of Stephen Leacock

Timothy Findley

The following is the introduction to a speech Findley gave at a Leacock symposium held at the University of Ottawa in 1985. It was later published in Stephen Leacock: A Reappraisal, *edited by David Staines; that text is reproduced here.*

You may wonder why it is that I, who am the author of books with titles such as *The Wars* and *Famous Last Words*, *Not Wanted on the Voyage* and *The Last of the Crazy People*, am writing in celebration of Stephen Leacock. The name of Leacock, after all, is synonymous with laughter, while my name (if I have one) is synonymous with madness, mayhem, and Armageddon. If the connection between Professor Leacock and myself seems somewhat forced — to say the least — perhaps I can explain.

I have been living for the last twenty-one years on a farm just forty miles south of Orillia, where Leacock lived. But that is not the connection. On the other hand, there is some connection in the fact that the farm where I live is barely seventeen miles to the east of Sibbald's Point, where Stephen Leacock is buried. All one needs to know is that the burial site at Sibbald's Point and the homestead site at Orillia face each other on opposite sides of Lake Simcoe.

Now, it just so happens that, back in the days when Leacock was up there alive near Orillia, my *so-called* Grandfather Findley (the *so-called* will be explained when I come to the end of this connection) had his summer residence down near Sibbald's Point. If they had possessed the right kind of telescopes, they could have seen each other fishing. But that is not the connection.

The next thing one needs to know, in order to make the connection between myself and Stephen Leacock, is about the graveyard at Sibbald's Point: the graveyard where Leacock is buried but where my *so-called* Grandfather Findley is *not* buried: *not* buried, because he *refused* to be buried there. Perhaps with good reason, from his point of view — again, as you will see when I come to the end of this.

The connection continues. In the graveyard at Sibbald's Point, where my *so-called* Grandfather Findley refused to be buried, lie not only the remains of Stephen Butler Leacock, but also the remains of little Maisie Roach, otherwise known as *Mazo de la Roche*.

Now, what follows is of immense importance. What is it that is wrong with Canadian literary sleuths that they have failed to discover, and therefore have failed to reveal, the story of the love affair between Mazo de la Roche and Stephen Leacock?

Do they think it is by pure and simple chance these two are buried within kissing-distance of one another? Well, let me tell you, it is not by chance.

For anyone who cares to think about it, the *grande affaire* between Stephen Leacock and Mazo de la Roche is as plain as the nose on Cyrano's face. The trouble is — and has been for far too long — that nobody *has* cared to think about it. And, therefore, our great Canadian literary sleuths have missed the multitude of clues that are virtually massed before them, for all to see, in the works of both Leacock and de la Roche.

Consider: *Jalna*, where Mazo's Whiteoaks family lives, and *Mariposa*, where Stephen's best-known characters live, are both on the shores of a lake.

Consider: the year 1912. It was in that year that old Granny Whiteoaks had all her teeth removed. And it was also in that year that Stephen Leacock's pen gave birth to all the citizens of *Mariposa*. I ask you: is this not Cadmus sowing the dragon's teeth in order to create a whole new race of men?

Well, one could go on and on and on. The references are legion....

How many readers are aware that *Jalna* is the word for *butterfly* in an obscure Hindi dialect?

How many readers are aware that *Mariposa* is the word for *butterfly* in Spanish?

How many readers are aware that early in my acting career, I played the role of Peter Pupkin on television, in a weekly series adapted from Stephen Leacock's *Sunshine Sketches of a Little Town* — his tales of *Mariposa*?

How many readers are aware that, later, in the early years of my writing career I adapted Mazo de la Roche's Jalna epic for television?

How many readers are aware that the title of my second novel is *The Butterfly Plague*?

One last question:

How many readers are now aware of why it was my *so-called* Grandfather Findley refused to be buried in the graveyard at Sibbald's Point along with Mazo de la Roche and Stephen Butler Leacock?

This is what I have always suspected. Because the man I knew as Grandfather Findley *refused* to be buried along with Stephen Leacock and Mazo de la Roche, it is my firm belief that he had some connection with their hitherto unknown liaison, and whatever that connection may have been, given all the literary clues, I can only conclude that I am *not* descended from Thomas Findley, but from that unsuspected and illicit union of literary giants.

Here before you is none other than the grandson of Stephen Leacock!

NOTES

1. All such citations from friends, family members, and associates come from the Mazo de la Roche Collection, Thomas Fisher Rare Book Library, University of Toronto, unless otherwise indicated. Included in this collection, as well, are Ronald Hambleton's taped interviews with various people who knew Mazo; I quote from these interviews throughout this book.

2. See Fellows for development of Jalna's Loyalist symbolism.

3. A letter from Mazo to her close friend Anne (Warnock) Dimock reads: "Then the train, Trafalgar Square, the lions, the Houses of Parliament, Buckingham Palace, bang, bang, bang, one after the other, like so many explosions. Think, my mind had been cradled there, and I had never seen it before" (qtd. in Hambleton, *Mazo de la Roche*). The passage in *Finch's Fortune* reads: "Westminster Bridge, the Houses of Parliament, Trafalgar Square, the lions, Buckingham Palace! They thundered at him like a series of explosions. It was too much. It was overwhelming."

4. As chieftain of the clan, Renny is linked to the very title of Sir James George Frazer's *The Golden Bough*: he is the priestly King of the Wood, enjoying the privilege of plucking the Golden Bough from a tree in the sacred grove. The oak is, of course, a sacred tree, worshipped, Frazer tells us, "by all the main branches of the Aryan stock in Europe," and associated with the highest god by both the Greeks and the Romans. The Druids esteemed the oak above all; their very name means "oak men." Robert Graves observes in *The White Goddess* that the oak is "the tree of endurance and triumph . . . said to 'court the lightning flash,'" adding that the oak's roots are believed "to extend as deep underground as its branches rise in the air — Virgil mentions this — which makes it emblematic of a god whose law runs both in Heaven and in the Underworld."

5. See Bell. Citing in a note a passage from *The Centennial of the Settlement of Upper Canada*, he suggests that the Loyalist confusion of patriotism with loyalism "led to the retention of symbols of colonial status to serve as symbols of national status. Not only did this confusion inhibit expression of the uniqueness of Canada and the development of Canadian (as opposed to British) identity, but it also accentuated a kind of social and cultural provincialism, manifested in the continuous aspiration, especially among the elite, to be recognized and accepted in England."

CHRONOLOGY

1879	On 15 January, Mazo Louise de la Roche is born Mazo Roche in Newmarket, Ontario, the only child of William R. and Alberta Roche. Mazo's gravestone gives 1888 as her year of birth (though she repeatedly claims it is 1885, and refers to Toronto as her birthplace).
1882	The family moves to nearby Aurora, where W.R. Roche becomes manager of his brother's general store.
1885	The Roches join the rest of William's family in Toronto; they move from there to Galt, Ontario, in the early 1890s.
1894	Mazo's parents move to Toronto's Parkdale district, where they live at 157 Dunn Avenue, home of Mazo's maternal grandparents. Caroline Clement, a cousin once removed, joins the family, and, with a few brief exceptions, remains with Mazo until the latter's death.
1900	Grandfather Daniel Lundy dies, resulting in the breakup of the Parkdale household.
1902	Mazo's first published short story, "The Thief of St. Loo," appears in *Munsey's Magazine*.
1903	Mazo experiences her first nervous breakdown.
1905	W.R. Roche becomes proprietor of a hotel in Acton, Ontario, which will provide Mazo with material not only for some short stories but also for her novel *Delight*.
1911	The Roches take up farming near Bronte, Ontario, the setting of *Possession*. The farm is named Rochedale.
1914	Mazo gives her terminally ill father his last Christmas present, the Scottish terrier Bunty, as the family prepares to leave Rochedale for Oakville, Ontario.
1915	W.R. Roche dies; the three women remove to Toronto.

1920	Alberta Roche dies of influenza.
1922	*Explorers of the Dawn*, a collection of short stories written during the previous decade, is published.
1923	*Possession*, Mazo's first novel, appears in February.
1924	Mazo and Caroline move into Trail Cottage, where they spend their next four summers.
1925	*Low Life*, a one-act play, is produced at Trinity Memorial Hall in Montreal. It wins first prize in competitions held by the IODE and the Montreal branch of the Canadian Author's Association, which also awards her play *Come True* an honourable mention.
1926	Mazo finishes *Jalna* and sees the publication of *Delight*; she and Caroline move to a flat at 86 Yorkville Avenue, Toronto.
1927	*Jalna* wins the ten-thousand-dollar *Atlantic*–Little, Brown Award in April. *Come True* is produced at Toronto's Hart House Theatre.
1928	Following Bunty's death the previous Christmas, Mazo suffers a second nervous breakdown and a six-month writer's block. Her play *The Return of the Emigrant* is produced at the Hart House Theatre.
1929	In the glow of the success of *Jalna*, Mazo and Caroline head for Europe in January; after spending six weeks in Naples and nearly three months in Taormina (the Sicilian town that supplies the backdrop for *Lark Ascending*), they visit London, arriving in Devon in May, only to depart immediately for the Cornish coast, Worcester, and Oxford. Winter finds them at Seckington, Winkleigh, Devon, enjoying the critical acclaim for *Whiteoaks of Jalna*.
1930	*Portrait of a Dog*, the story of Bunty, is published.
1931	Mazo and Caroline visit Europe and adopt a young girl and boy; they furnish The Rectory, Hawkchurch, Devon, the setting of *Beside a Norman Tower* (1932). The third of the Jalna novels, *Finch's Fortune*, appears.
1932	*Lark Ascending* is published; at the end of the year the family moves to Stafford Place, London.
1933	After moving the family back to Devon, Mazo decides

	they will sail to Canada, where they stay at Springfield Farm in Erindale, Ontario. Caroline is injured in an automobile accident and then breaks her leg, and so they winter at Castle Frank Road in Toronto. *The Master of Jalna* appears, and *The Thunder of New Wings* is serialized in *Chatelaine*.
1934	Mazo, Caroline, and children cross the Atlantic again, this time to live at The Winnings, in the Cotswolds, where Mazo works on *Young Renny*.
1935	*Young Renny* is completed; RKO releases the film *Jalna* in August.
1936	A bumper year: *Whiteoak Harvest* is published and *Whiteoaks* is produced on stage in London. It stars Nancy Price as Adeline Whiteoak, and runs for three years (it is later produced in Canada and the United States, with Ethel Barrymore as Gran).
1937	*The Very House*, begun in 1935, is published, and helps pay for Vale House, in Clewer, near Windsor Castle.
1938	The family summers on the Cornish coast as *Growth of a Man*, based on the life of Mazo's cousin H.R. MacMillan, wealthy British Columbia lumberman and entrepreneur, is published. Mazo is awarded the Lorne Pierce Medal for distinguished contribution to Canadian literature.
1939	Mazo, Caroline, and the children sail for North America, eventually settling at Windrush Hill in York Mills, north of Toronto. The publication of *The Sacred Bullock and Other Stories of Animals* marks their return.
1940	*Whiteoak Heritage*, the seventh of the Jalna novels, appears; it is followed by *Wakefield's Course* (1941), *The Building of Jalna* (1944), *Return to Jalna* (1946), *Mary Wakefield* (1949), *Renny's Daughter* (1951), *Whiteoak Brothers* (1953), *Variable Winds at Jalna* (1954), *Centenary at Jalna* (1958), and *Morning at Jalna* (1960).
1942	*The Two Saplings* appears in England and Canada, but not in the United States. The CBC broadcasts the radio serial *Jalna* in nine weekly episodes beginning in March.
1945	*Quebec: Historic Seaport* is published as part of Doubleday's Seaport Series.

1946	The family moves to the village of Forest Hill (now part of Toronto), and Trail Cottage is sold.
1951	*The Mistress of Jalna*, based on *Mary Wakefield*, appears on stage in England and Canada; Mazo travels to Banff to accept the University of Alberta's first University National Award Medal for her career contribution to Canadian letters.
1952	*A Boy in the House and Other Stories* is published; Mazo and Caroline make their final move, to 3 Ava Crescent in Forest Hill.
1954	Mazo is awarded an honorary doctorate by the University of Toronto. The first instalment of the five-episode production *Young Renny*, part of the BBC program *Sunday's Play*, begins on 5 December, followed, at intervals of six weeks, by *Whiteoak Heritage*, *Jalna*, *The Building of Jalna*, and *Whiteoaks*.
1955	Mazo's children's book *The Song of Lambert* appears.
1956	The BBC broadcasts *The Building of Jalna* as part of its *Book at Bedtime* readings series.
1957	*Ringing the Changes*, the autobiography Mazo has begun in 1954, appears, and is perhaps most notable for its omissions.
1958	A second children's book, *Bill and Coo*, is published.
1959	*Mary Wakefield* and *Young Renny* are aired as serial readings on the BBC's *Women's Hour*.
1961	Mazo de la Roche dies on 12 July, at home in Forest Hill.
1966	Ronald Hambleton's biography, *Mazo de la Roche of Jalna*, is published.
1970	As part of Twayne's World Authors Series, George Hendrick publishes a critical-analytical study, *Mazo de la Roche*.
1972	The broadcast of the thirteen-part CBC Television series *The Whiteoaks of Jalna* ironically heralds the demise of Mazo's popularity. Caroline Clement dies.
1984	René de la Roche, Mazo's adopted son, dies. He is buried near his mother's and Caroline's graves in the St. George's churchyard at Sibbald Point.
1989	Joan Givner reassesses the Mazo de la Roche canon from a feminist perspective in her *Mazo de la Roche: The Hidden Life*.

1994   *Jalna*, a sixteen-million-dollar series produced by France 2, enjoys immense popularity when it premiers on television.

WORKS CITED

Acton's Early Days. Acton: Acton Free Press, 1939.
Andrews, Bernadette. "Jalna: The Famous Old House Is Saved from Wreckers." *Toronto Star* 6 Jan. 1975: D1.
Beaton, Joyce. "Famous Author Found Privacy at *The Briars*." *Early Canadian Life* May 1978: n. pag.
Bell, David V. "The Loyalist Tradition in Canada." *Journal of Canadian Studies* 5.2 (1970): 22–33.
Bly, Robert. *Iron John: A Book About Men.* Reading, MA: Addison-Wesley, 1990.
Byers, Mary, and Margaret McBurney. *The Governor's Road: Early Buildings and Families from Mississauga to London.* Toronto: U of Toronto P, 1982.
Byers, Mary, et al. *Rural Roots: Pre-Confederation Buildings of the York Region of Ontario.* Toronto: U of Toronto P, 1976.
Daymond, Douglas. "Lark Ascending." *Canadian Literature* 81 (1981): 172–78.
———. "Mazo de la Roche's Forgotten Novel." *Journal of Canadian Fiction* 3.2: 55–59.
———. "Whiteoak Chronicles: A Reassessment." *Canadian Literature* 66 (1975): 48–62.
de la Roche, Mazo. *Beside a Norman Tower.* Toronto: Macmillan, 1934.
———. *Bill and Coo.* Toronto: Macmillan, 1958.
———. *A Boy in the House.* London: Macmillan, 1952.
———. *A Boy in the House and Other Stories.* Boston: Macmillan, 1952.
———. *The Building of Jalna.* Boston: Little, 1944.
———. *Centenary at Jalna.* London: Macmillan, 1958.
———. *Come True.* Toronto: Macmillan, 1927.
———. *Delight.* Toronto: Macmillan, 1926.
———. *Explorers of the Dawn.* 1922. Toronto: Macmillan: 1923.
———. *Finch's Fortune.* 1931. Toronto: Macmillan, 1933.
———. *Growth of a Man.* Boston: Little, 1938.
———. "I Still Remember." *Maclean's* 27 Apr. 1957: 15+.
———. *Jalna.* 1927. Toronto: Macmillan, 1929.
———. *Lark Ascending.* Toronto: Macmillan, 1932.
———. *Low Life.* Toronto: Macmillan, 1925.
———. *Mary Wakefield.* Boston: Little, 1949.

———. *The Master of Jalna*. London: Macmillan, 1933.
———. *Morning at Jalna*. London: Macmillan, 1960.
———. "My First Book." *Canadian Author and Bookman* 28 (1952): 3–4.
———. *Portrait of a Dog*. London: Macmillan, 1930.
———. *Possession*. Toronto: Macmillan, 1923.
———. *Quebec: Historic Seaport*. Seaport Series. Garden City, NY: Doubleday, 1944.
———. *Renny's Daughter*. London: Macmillan, 1951.
———. *The Return of the Emigrant*. Boston: Little, 1929.
———. *Return to Jalna*. Toronto: Macmillan, 1946.
———. *Ringing the Changes*. Toronto: Macmillan, 1957.
———. *The Sacred Bullock and Other Stories of Animals*. Toronto: Macmillan, 1939.
———. *Selected Stories of Mazo de la Roche*. Ed. Douglas Daymond. Canadian Short Story Library. Ottawa: U of Ottawa P, 1979.
———. *The Song of Lambert*. Toronto: Macmillan, 1955.
———. *The Thunder of New Wings*. *Chatelaine* June 1933–Feb. 1934.
———. *The Two Saplings*. London: Macmillan, 1942.
———. *Variable Winds at Jalna*. Toronto: Macmillan, 1954.
———. *The Very House*. Boston: Little, 1937.
———. *Wakefield's Course*. Boston: Little, 1941.
———. *The Whiteoak Brothers: Jalna — 1923*. Toronto: Macmillan, 1953.
———. *Whiteoak Harvest*. 1936. Toronto: Macmillan, 1948.
———. *Whiteoak Heritage*. 1940. London: Macmillan, 1947.
———. *Whiteoaks: A Play*. Boston: Little, 1936.
———. *Whiteoaks of Jalna*. 1929. Boston: Little, 1957.
———. "The Winnings: Our Home in the Cotswolds." *Arts and Decoration* Jan. 1937: 23–27.
———. *Young Renny*. Toronto: Macmillan, 1935.
"de la Roche, Mazo." *Twentieth Century Authors: A Biographical Dictionary of Modern Literature*. 1942 ed.
"de la Roche, Mazo." *Twentieth Century Authors: A Biographical Dictionary of Modern Literature*. 1st supp. 1955.
De Salvo, Louise. *Virginia Woolf: The Impact of Childhood Sexual Abuse on Her Life and Work*. Boston: Beacon, 1989.
Dills, K. Telephone interview. 11 Oct. 1994.
Duffy, Dennis. *Gardens, Covenants, Exiles: Loyalism in the Literature of Upper Canada/Ontario*. Toronto: U of Toronto P, 1982.
Edward Weeks Papers. Harry Ransome Humanities Research Center. University of Texas, Austin.
Fellows, Jo-Ann. "The 'British Connection' in the Jalna Novels of Mazo de la Roche: The Loyalist Myth Revisited." *Dalhousie Review* 56 (1976): 283–90.
Finch, Robert. Telephone interview. 24 Aug. 1994.
Findley, Timothy. *National Treasures*. With June Callwood. Vision TV, Toronto. 16 Apr. 1992.

———. "Riding Off in All Directions: A Few Wild Words in Search of Stephen Leacock." *Stephen Leacock: A Reappraisal*. Re-Appraisals: Canadian Writers 12. Ed. David Staines. Ottawa: U of Ottawa P, 1986. 5–9.

———. *The Wars*. Toronto: Clarke, 1977.

Frazer, Sir James George. *The Golden Bough: A Study in Magic and Religion*. abr. ed. New York: Macmillan, 1947.

Frye, Northrop. *The Bush Garden: Essays on the Canadian Imagination*. Toronto: Anansi, 1971.

———. Introduction. *The Great Code: The Bible and Literature*. Toronto: Academic, 1982. xi–xxiii.

Genealogies of the Builders of the Sharon Temple. 3rd ed. Sharon, ON: Sharon Temple, 1994.

Givner, Joan. *Mazo de la Roche: The Hidden Life*. Toronto: Oxford UP, 1989.

Graves, Robert. *The White Goddess*. London: Faber, 1948.

Hale, Katherine. "Joan of the Barnyard — A Young Poetess Who Loves Chickens." *Star Weekly* 7 Feb. 1914: 1.

Hambleton, Ronald. *Mazo de la Roche of Jalna*. New York: Hawthorn, 1966.

———. *The Secret of Jalna*. Toronto: General, 1972.

Hendrick, George. *Mazo de la Roche*. Twayne's World Authors Series 129. New York: Twayne, 1970.

Larson, Barbara. Personal interviews. 1992–96.

Lawrence, D.H. "Edgar Allan Poe." *Selected Literary Criticism*. Ed. Anthony Beal. New York: Viking, 1956. 330–46.

Livesay, Dorothy. "The Making of Jalna: A Reminiscence." *Canadian Literature* 23 (1965): 25–30.

———. "Mazo Explored." *Canadian Literature* 32 (1967): 57–59.

———. "Remembering Mazo" [foreword]. De La Roche, *Selected Stories* 11–13.

Mazo de la Roche Collection. Thomas Fisher Rare Book Library, University of Toronto.

Metcalf, George. "William Henry Draper." *The Pre-Confederation Premiers: Ontario Government Leaders, 1841–1867*. Ed. J.M.S. Careless. Toronto: U of Toronto P, 1980. 32–88.

Pacey, Desmond. Introduction. *Delight*. By Mazo de la Roche. New Canadian Library 21. Toronto: McClelland, 1961. vii–x.

Pringle, Gertrude. "Miss Mazo de la Roche: Canadian Novelist and Coming Playwright." *Saturday Night* 29 Jan. 1927: 21.

———. "World Fame to Canadian Author." *Canadian Magazine* 67 (1927): 19+.

Rees, Esmée. Personal interview. 25 Aug. 1994.

Rouyer, Charles-Antoine. "Mazo de la Roche." *L'Express* 20–26 Aug. 1994: 1+.

Sandwell, B.K. "Canadian Authors' Association." *Canadian Bookman* June 1927: 186–87.

Snell, J.G. "The United States at Jalna." *Canadian Literature* 66 (1975): 31–40.

Tyrrell, Marjorie. Telephone interview. 27 July 1994.

"Was Toronto Home 'Jalna'?: Authoress Left 30-Year Riddle." *Telegram* [Toronto] 13 July 1961: 20.

INDEX

Acton, ON 23, 35, 45–46, 49–50, 58, 60, 64, 65–67, 135
Acton Free Press 45
Acton's Early Days 66
Arts and Letters Club (Toronto) 97
Atlantic Monthly 15, 30, 34, 49, 60, 80, 86–87, 90, 97, 100, 151
Aurora, ON 23, 38

Barrymore, Ethel 122
Beardmore family (Acton) 66
Bell, David 137–38
Benares (Clarkson) 68, 71–72, 75, 76, 77–78, 80, 82, 86, 89, 167
Beverley (Beardmore house) 66, 73, 74
Boney (parrot) 121–22
Boston 22, 129
Briars, The (Jackson's Point) 35, 73, 75, 153
Bronte, ON (Grimstone) 14, 23, 35, 45–46, 48–50, 56–57, 58–60, 67, 130
Bryan, Abraham (Uncle Bryan) 42
Bryan, Sarah Danford (Mazo's great-grandmother) 28, 89
Bryan family 24
Bunty 67, 80–81, 87, 97, 123
  death of 68, 98
Bush Garden, The (Frye) 25, 62

CBC (television series: *The Whiteoaks of Jalna*) 77, 153–64

Canadian Magazine 35
Castle Frank Road (Toronto) 112, 119
Chatelaine 15, 112
Clarkson, ON 14, 16, 23, 69, 78–86, 87, 123, 140, 154
Clemency, Dr. Morgan 21
Clemens, Samuel (Mark Twain) 51, 126
Clement, Caroline 14–16, 24–26, 29–30, 32–34, 37–39, 42–47, 49, 51, 54, 61, 67–69, 71, 75, 78–81, 85, 87, 90, 94, 96–103, 107, 110, 111–12, 119, 121, 123, 126, 129, 140, 149–50, 153, 155, 163, 166
Cudmore, Bill 50, 58–59
Cudmore, Jack 58–59
Custom of the Country, The (Wharton) 108

Daymond, Douglas 146
Deacon, William Arthur 55
de la Roche, René 52, 79–80, 84, 85, 111, 114, 123, 129, 134, 144, 166
DeSalvo, Louise 37
Devon 25, 101, 105
Dills, Mrs. K. 45
Doubleday 133
Draper, George 71
Draper, William Henry 71, 85
Duffy, Dennis 135
Dunn Avenue (Toronto) 42, 47
Eildon Hall (Jackson's Point) 73, 153, 167

Elmhurst, Mrs. Richard 45

Fairy Lake (Acton) 60, 64, 66
Fairy Lake (Newmarket) 21, 22, 23
Fellows, Jo-Ann 25, 143
Finch, Robert 16, 104
Findley, Timothy 13, 17, 45, 63, 72, 75, 99, 122, 153–64, 168–70
Forest Hill, ON (Toronto) 23, 65, 140, 145, 149
France 2 Network (*Jalna* series) 149
Frye, Northrop 13, 25, 62, 92

Galt, ON (Cambridge) 23, 28, 36, 39–41, 43
Genealogies of the Builders of the Sharon Temple 29
Georgian Bay (Ontario) 23, 34, 97
Givner, Joan 13, 15, 30, 44, 56, 147, 149
Gods Arrive, The (Wharton) 106
Golden Bowl, The (James) 107
Great Code, The (Frye) 13

Hagan, Annemarie 71
Hale, Katherine 72
Hambleton, Ronald 13, 16, 24, 27, 43, 45–46, 50, 56, 59, 73, 78, 111, 115, 133–35
Harper's Bazaar 106
Harris, Anne (and Beverley Sayers) 69, 78–79, 148
Harris, Arthur 80, 91
Harris, James 71
Harris, James Beveridge (Captain) 71, 75, 78, 88, 91
Harris, John (Major General) 88, 89
Harris, Naomi 78
Harris family 69, 71–72, 78, 144, 153 (see also Sayers family)
Hawkchurch (The Rectory) 109, 112, 119

Hendrick, George 13, 30, 46
High Park (Toronto) 23
Hollywood 119

Iron John (Bly) 115

Jackson's Point, ON 73, 153

Knopf, Alfred 48

Lake Joseph (Muskoka) 55
Lake Simcoe 23, 34–35, 67–68, 153, 166, 169
Larson, Barbara Sayers 16, 78–86, 123, 140
Leacock, Stephen 133, 154, 164, 168–70
Lévi-Strauss, Claude 13
Little, Brown 87, 100, 106, 132–33
Livesay, Dorothy 63, 69, 71, 80–82, 90
Livesay, Florence 69, 80
Livesay, J.F.B. 69, 80
London 101, 111, 119–23
Lovat Dickson, H.H. (Rache) 24, 152
Lundy, Alberta (see Roche)
Lundy, Daniel Ambrose (grandfather) 21, 27, 37–38, 40, 43, 150
Lundy, Emily (Aunt Eva) 32, 38, 46–47, 51, 68, 130
Lundy, Frank (uncle) 15, 43
Lundy, George (uncle) 30
Lundy, Dr. John 27
Lundy, Sylvester 25
Lundy, Walter (uncle) 130
Lundy family 24–26, 38, 42, 96, 124, 136

MacKenzie, Jean 73
Macmillan Company, The, of Canada 148

Macmillan Company, The, of London 24, 147, 152
Macmillan Company, The, of New York 87
Macmillan, Daniel 111, 118
Macmillan, Harold 111
Macmillan, H.R. (Reggie) 24, 124, 127
Magrath family 85, 91–92
Malvern (The Winnings) 111
Mansbendel, Pierre 46–47, 68, 130, 150
Massey, Raymond 119
Massey family 72
Mazo de la Roche of Jalna (Hambleton) 50, 67, 118, 121–22, 124
McIntyre, Alfred 77
Morley, Christopher 48–49, 55, 100
Munsey's Magazine 44

New England 23
Newmarket, ON 14, 21, 22, 23–24, 27–28, 38, 46, 49, 123–24
North York, ON (Toronto) 130
Nova Scotia 23, 69

Oakville, ON 23, 58, 130, 141
Osler, E.F. (Major) 59

Parkdale, ON (Toronto) 23, 32, 33, 96
Patterson, Dr. Bradford 20
Patterson, Mrs. B. (Fanny Bryan) 20
Pointe-au-Baril, ON 45
Price, Nancy 119–22

Quebec 23
Queen Elizabeth II 148
Queen Mary 121–22, 148–49

Rees, Mrs. Esmée 16, 30, 52, 63, 65, 79–80, 84, 85, 111, 114, 117, 129
Reid, George Agnew 45

Richmond Hill, ON 23
Roche, Alberta Lundy (Mazo's mother) 14, 21, 28, 37–38, 41–43, 46, 55, 67, 98, 103, 150
   death of 54
Roche, Danford 38, 43, 52
Roche, Francis 27, 98
Roche, John Richmond (Mazo's grandfather) 27
Roche, Mazo de la
   animals and nature, love of 14, 29, 39–40, 47, 50, 55–56, 62, 67–68, 94, 103, 108, 145
   death of 49, 149
   drawings 31, 32
   grave 166
   hands 149–52
   myth (importance of) 25
   nervous breakdowns 28–29, 34, 37, 44, 95–98, 128
   oak (symbolism) 23
   play, the 29–30, 32–34, 51, 97, 116, 126
   works of
      Beside a Norman Tower 109, 111–13, 147
      Bill and Coo 145
      Boy in the House, A 68, 131
      Building of Jalna, The 135–38
      Centenary at Jalna 34, 89, 145–46, 155
      Come True 63
      Delight 46, 58, 60–63, 66, 67, 93, 118, 124
      Explorers of the Dawn 26, 47–54, 55, 69, 100
      "Father, The" 148
      Finch's Fortune 100–05, 117
      Growth of a Man 20, 27, 63, 119, 123–29, 130
      Jalna 16, 26, 28, 43, 55, 67, 71, 72, 75, 77, 80–82, 86–87, 90, 92–95, 97, 100, 105–06,

183

118–19, 143, 147, 158
Lark Ascending 100–01,
    106–08, 126
Low Life 63
Mary Wakefield 43, 140
Master of Jalna, The 85, 89,
    104, 115–17, 148
Morning at Jalna 136, 147
"My First Book" 52, 69
Portrait of a Dog 67–68, 112, 130
Possession 48, 50, 55–58, 59–63,
    67, 93, 102–03, 118, 124
"Quartet" 106
Quebec: Historic Seaport 119,
    133–35
Renny's Daughter 139–40, 141
Return of the Emigrant, The 63
Return to Jalna 103–04, 138–40
Ringing the Changes 15, 21, 23,
    24–26, 29–30, 32, 35–36,
    42–48, 50–52, 55, 58, 69, 75,
    86–87, 89, 95, 97–98,
    100–03, 112, 118–19, 125–27,
    129, 131, 134, 149–50, 151, 152,
    158
*Sacred Bullock and Other Stories
    of Animals, The* 40, 112
"Son of a Miser, The" 44
Song of Lambert, The 145
"Spirit of the Dance, The"
    35–36, 40–41
"Thief of St. Loo, The" 44
Thunder of New Wings, The 15,
    112, 150
Two Saplings, The 132
Variable Winds at Jalna 142–43
Very House, The 54, 111–13, 147
Wakefield's Course 104, 131–32
*Whiteoak Brothers: Jalna —
    1923* 43, 139, 141–42
Whiteoak Chronicles 118
Whiteoak Harvest 104, 115, 118,
    130–31
Whiteoak Heritage 47–48, 68,
    129–30
Whiteoaks (the play) 45, 87, 89,
    115, 119, 120, 121–23, 131–32,
    149
Whiteoaks of Jalna 87, 89,
    93–99, 105, 107, 119, 153
Young Renny 43, 115, 117–19
Roche, Sarah Bryan (Mazo's
    grandmother) 42, 89, 96
Roche, William Richmond (Mazo's
    father) 14, 23, 28–29, 33, 36–38,
    42–48, 52, 58–60, 65, 67, 89, 96,
    103, 127
    death of 48, 150
Russell Hill Road (Forest Hill) 140

St. George's (Sibbald Memorial)
    Church 164, 165, 166
St. Peter's Anglican Church
    (Erindale) 91, 92
Sandwell, B.K. (see *Saturday Night*)
Saturday Night 55, 124, 147
Sayers, Beverley (see Harris, Anne)
Sayers, Mr. and Mrs. Geoffrey
    77–78
Sayers family 78 (see also Harris
    family)
Sedgwick, Ellery 87, 117, 134
Sharon Temple 125, 126
Sibbald family 73, 75, 153–54,
    164–65, 167–70
Skynner family 82
    Skynner house (The Anchorage)
    82, 83
Snell, J.G. 142
Sovereign House (Oakville) 167
Staines, David 168
Stone, Reverend C.H. 115

Trail Cottage (Clarkson) 14, 46, 60,
    67–69, 70, 71, 80, 85, 87, 90, 98,
    104, 123, 140

Tyrrell, Mrs. Marjorie (Cudmore) 58–59

United Empire Loyalists 25–27, 71, 93, 122–23, 133, 135–39, 143, 145–49

Vale House (Windsor) 25, 123, 129, 140

Wars, The (Findley) 13, 99, 157, 161
Weeks, Edward 30, 34, 106, 117–18, 129, 148, 151, 152
Weeks, Edward, papers 15
Willson, Hiram (Mazo's great-grandfather) 25, 124, 126
Willson family 24, 27, 124, 126
Windrush Hill (North York) 130, 140
Windsor, England 26
Winnings, The (Cotswolds) 123
Woodlot (Clarkson) 69
Woolf, Virginia 37
Wrong, George M. 44

York Mills, ON (Toronto) 23
Yorkville, ON (Toronto) 23, 90, 97